NEWMAN

PAUL

NEWMAN

A BIOGRAPHY

NEWMAN

PAUL

NEWMAN

A BIOGRAPHY

ERIC LAX

Turner Publishing, Inc.

ATLANTA

For my son Simon

Library of Congress Cataloging-in-Publication Data

Lax, Eric.

    Paul Newman: a biography/by Eric Lax.—1st ed.

      p.   cm.

    Filmography: p.

    Includes bibliographical references and index.

    ISBN 1-57036-286-6 (alk. paper)

    1. Newman, Paul, 1925– . 2. Motion picture actors and actresses—United

States—Biography. 1. Title

PN2287. N44L38 1996

791. 43'028'092—dc20

[B]   95–49018

                                                CIP

Published by Turner Publishing, Inc.

A subsidiary of Turner Broadcasting System, Inc.

1050 Techwood Drive, N.W.

Atlanta, Georgia 30318

Distributed by Andrews and McMeel

A Universal Press Syndicate Company

4900 Main Street

Kansas City, Missouri 64112

10 9 8 7 6 5 4 3 2 1

First published in Great Britain in 1996 by Pavilion Books Limited

DESIGNED BY THE BRIDGEWATER BOOK COMPANY LIMITED

Typeset/Page make-up by Lee Forster

Picture research by Juliet Brightmore

Printed and bound in Singapore by Imago.

Turner Publishing, Inc.

CONTENTS

Were it not for a barroom brawl in Gambier, Ohio, in 1948, perhaps none of this would be important. Or so he says. Not that this one was particularly different from any of the regular mêlées that broke out on weekends between

Newman's Luck

students of all-male Kenyon College and town boys possessive of the local women. The bars and dance halls of that small community in central Ohio were about the

only places to find a date, and as demand always outweighed supply, disappointment was inevitable. Who punched whom would normally have been of little consequence, except that on this night the quarterback of the football team decked a plainclothes police officer—he wore no badge, *for heaven's sake; who was to know?—and before anyone realized who the guy on the floor was, several other players landed some punches too and the fight was on.*

LEFT
While making *Somebody Up There Likes Me* (1956). This was the second boxing role that Newman took over because of James Dean's death. He resisted taking them initially because "I didn't want to gain anything as the result of someone else's tragedy."

RIGHT
As a young man, Newman's face was as sculpted as an emperor's on an ancient coin. After graceful ageing, it now has the etched look of someone on a postage stamp.

Uniformed police arrived and broke things up. As they took him away with two of his teammates, the quarterback flipped his car keys to a 152-pound second-string linebacker and asked him to bring the car to the station. When he did, the desk sergeant asked to see his hands. One look at their red, swollen knuckles and he was locked up, too. An hour later, half the Kenyon student body was in the parking lot of the jail, singing old college songs and drinking beer. "I mean," the ex-linebacker said with a laugh one month before he turned seventy, "it was *wonderful*." The college thought it was less than that. The two main combatants were expelled and the linebacker and three others thrown off the team and put on probation.

So it was that Paul Newman became an actor. He wasn't much of a football player anyway. Or so he says. When he speaks, what comes out is not always a whole sentence but rather the heart of one: "Bad one. Really scrub team. Never amounted to much." Then the summation: "My ambition was always greater than my talent."

He was twenty-three years old and in college on the GI Bill. He had enlisted in the air branch of the Naval Reserve Officer Training Corps when he was seventeen, and immediately following his graduation from high school in January 1943 he spent four months at Ohio University in Athens while waiting to be called up. Now older and, he thought, wiser, he didn't want to go back to a coed school—"so that I could keep away from women." His intention was noble but his resolve was weak. "That lasted about ..." Here he breaks into a throaty chuckle and shakes his head. "Bad move." A laugh. "Poor choice."

It was difficult to have a major in women in an all-male school. For that matter, it was often difficult for him just to get to class, although he did manage to gain a degree in speech. But until his junior year when his banishment from football forced him to find another outlet for his enthusiasm, not to mention his drinking and fighting, "There's some question as to what direction I would have taken."

As it turned out, direction of another sort was something he has taken quite well. "I was a *terrible* student," he says with the easy self-effacement of someone who has excelled for the ensuing forty-five years. But not, it was immediately clear, a terrible actor. Although he says he was always "uncomfortable," he appeared in several elementary and high school productions, including at the age of twelve the starring role in the Cleveland Playhouse staging of *St. George and the Dragon*. During his short stay at Ohio University he had won the part of boxer Speed McFarland in the Lynn Root and Harry Clork comedy *The Milky Way*, but Kenyon was where he threw himself into acting. In his junior and senior years he had the lead in ten dramatic society productions ranging from *The Front Page* and *Charley's Aunt* to *The Taming of the Shrew* and *The Alchemist*. In fact James Michael, his drama professor, said some years ago that he had "trouble not casting Paul in the lead of every play." Plus Newman wrote, directed, starred in, and produced a musical. The root of his mediocre scholarship was simple: "I didn't have time for school."

He wasted no time getting away from it. Graduation exercises in June 1949 were over at 2 pm, and he says that at 3 pm he was on the train for Williams Bay, Wisconsin, and summer stock. Within five years he would appear on Broadway and be signed to a contract with Warner Bros. Within ten he would be an international star whose most persistent, characteristic role is that of a marginal American whose stubbornness and will generally defeat his best interests, but whose personal appeal wins our hearts. He is an anomaly, a hero who may get the girl along the way but almost never winds up with her in the end. For two generations now he has been an integral part of American popular culture. The parts of his body of work to date consist of three acclaimed roles on Broadway, fifty-three movies (four of which he directed), eight Academy Award nominations, and three Oscars (one for Best Actor, one honorary, and one for his humanitarian work). Cinema aside, there is his life-long liberal political activism and membership of the group of recent purchasers of the venerable and feisty left-of-center weekly magazine *The Nation*; a stint as a U. S. delegate to a 1978 United Nations session on disarmament; the number nineteen spot on Richard Nixon's enemies list; the four national amateur automobile racing championships; the second-place finish at the Le Mans 24-hour race in 1979; the first in-class and third overall finish at the 1995 Daytona 24-hour event—making him the oldest driver ever to win a professionally sanctioned motor race—and, of course, through it all the marriage of thirty-seven years and counting to Joanne Woodward. Oh, and this, too: since 1982 he's given away close to $70 million, all the post-tax profits from Newman's Own, the salad dressing, spaghetti sauce, lemonade, and popcorn business that began as a lark to raise a few bucks for charity. Some lark. "Newman's Luck," he says of virtually everything he does that succeeds. Some luck.

Arthur and Paul Newman. As children, Paul says, "belligerent, I think, is a good word" to describe the brothers' relationship. As adults, they are close. Arthur has been involved with the production of several of Paul's films.

We know him as Hud and Harper and Fast Eddie and Butch Cassidy and a dozen other names, but it is always dangerous to think that means we really know him, even if the advertisements did blare that "Paul Newman *is* Hud" or "Paul Newman *is* Harper." Paul Leonard Newman, born 26 January 1925 in Cleveland, Ohio, brings texture to the Paul Newman who is Hud or Harper or two score and ten others who were born in the minds of writers. *That* Paul Newman is those people. P. L. Newman, to use his racing name, takes something from himself and a lot from his imagination and breathes life into those characters on the screen. For all of that, life is lived as well as imagined, and there are places where the artist and his characters almost inevitably intersect. Yet however titillating this stereopticon view, Newman's achievement is that he makes his characters real to us regardless of any actual experience with them.

While he often plays men who have a lower-middle-class background, Newman and his year-older brother, Arthur, were raised in considerable comfort in a gracious eleven-room house in the leafy and affluent Cleveland suburb of Shaker Heights. He once said that "belligerent, I think, is a good word" to describe their relationship growing up, but as adults they have become close. "Fierce, fierce son of a bitch," Paul says of Arthur with evident admiration. Arthur, who has the same blue eyes and an alarmingly similar voice, has worked in varied production capacities on a number of Paul's movies, and recently Paul helped him in his successful campaign for the city council in Rancho Mirage, California, where, Newman says, Arthur "is raising all sorts of good hell."

Their father, Arthur S. Newman Sr., was a German-descended Jew. Their mother, Theresa Fetzer, was a Hungarian of Catholic descent who, for reasons unknown to Paul, became a Christian Scientist when he was five. Even so, Arthur and Paul had regular medical check-ups. None of these varied religious beliefs stuck to Paul, although he has said that he considers himself a Jew "because it is more challenging."

Arthur Sr. and his brother, Joseph, were partners in the Newman-Stern Company, a prosperous sporting goods company in Cleveland. Before starting the company in 1915, they had both been journalists—Joseph was a well-known newspaper writer around Ohio and in the 1950s published such books of whimsical verse as *Perishable Poems* and *Poems for Penguins*; Arthur at seventeen was the youngest reporter ever hired by the *Cleveland Press* but soon left to join Joe at the store, where they put in six-day weeks. Both brothers apparently had a wonderful sense of humour, but what most struck Paul about his father was his sense of ethics and morals. As a businessman he had such an impeccable reputation for paying his bills that even during the Depression major companies sent him hundreds of thousands of dollars' worth of goods on consignment. That sense of rectitude carried over into how he treated his sons. No matter that your father owned a store full of balls and gloves and the various accoutrements of games: you earned the privilege of possessing its goods. Paul did not get his first baseball mitt until he was ten, an event he has approvingly called "a lesson." The other side of that strictness and the long hours at work was that father and son were distanced, a breach Paul has blamed largely on himself.

"I didn't know what was going on, either with myself or with the outside world," he has said. "I don't think he had the patience to deal with things in a superfluous way—which … is not a criticism of him. It's really a criticism of myself. I was a late bloomer. I didn't have any idea of what being close to an older person was until much later in life."

Newman c. 1950, when he returned to Cleveland after his father's death to help manage the family sporting goods business.

Rather than being blown up, he grew up—six inches in one year to his present 5 feet 10 inches. Still, he says, he was so youthful that "I got through the whole war on two razor blades." He entered Kenyon in the fall of 1946, intending to concentrate on business and economics, but he soon switched to literature and drama. And beer; he claims that he was graduated with Magna Cum Lager honors. To earn extra money he ran a student laundry on the main street in town, and to attract business he bought a keg of beer every Saturday morning for the fellows to drink while their clothes were being washed and dried. He cleared $250–$300 a month. Just before graduation he sold the goodwill of the business to an underclassman. And here he invokes his luck again.

Horses were still common in town, and one Saturday, some time after the beer had been tapped, a stallion was standing near the laundry. One student, whose senses were seemingly in the washer with his shirts, put on boxing gloves and was apprehended in the act of helping the horse achieve sexual satisfaction. The laundry was shut down the next day. It is only good fortune, Newman feels, that prevented such a thing happening during his ownership.

But he was long gone by then, off for summer stock and graduated, if not with distinction, at least graduated. "I think they were generous to me," he says. "I think a lot of my grades were below average, but then enough were above average that they just said, 'Why don't we just give the guy four C's and let him get out of here?'" If that was indeed the case, it was a smarter move on Kenyon's part than they knew at the time. Through the 1970s Newman returned to work with their drama department, and his name is a high-profile association for an excellent but low-profile school. In 1981 the college put aside any notion of past grades and awarded him an honorary degree of Doctor of Humane Letters. He was off probation for good.

In Williams Bay, Wisconsin, that summer he appeared in the Norman Krasna comedy *John Loves Mary* and as the Gentleman Caller in Tennessee Williams's *The Glass Menagerie*, the first of his career-long associations with Williams's work. Immediately thereafter he was invited to sign on for the 1949–50 season with the Woodstock Players, a repertory company based near Chicago. It was a busy year. He appeared in sixteen successive plays; among his roles was Christian de Neuvilette, the handsome but stupid lover of Roxane for whom Cyrano supplies the eloquence in Rostand's *Cyrano de Bergerac*. In real life, he became the handsome

but intelligent husband of Jacqueline Witte, a lively blonde member of the company with a good sense of humor, five years younger than he. She was pregnant with their first child when Paul's father died in May 1950 at the age of fifty-seven. Paul quit the company and returned to Shaker Heights, bought a house, and settled in to help run the store.

So much was unresolved: a career just beginning, a family just starting, a stunted relationship that could now never grow. There is some irony and echo here; thirty-five years earlier, Paul's father had left his promising job at the *Cleveland Press* to enter the family business. Now it was his turn.

The theme of unhappy or unresolved relations between father and son (actual and allegorical) is at the heart of many of Newman's movies, from early ones such as *The Rack*, through *Cat on a Hot Tin Roof*, *From the Terrace* and *Hud*, to 1994's *Nobody's Fool*, in which this time he is the father. The pain of irresolution and loss is something he tragically knows too well, as a son and as a father. Newman's son Scott, with whom he apparently had an uneasy relationship, died at the age of twenty-eight from an accidental overdose of drugs and alcohol. *Nobody's Fool*, which is about a heretofore emotionally inaccessible father becoming accessible to his son, provides the most satisfying resolution of any of his films. Perhaps that's because this is one movie in which Newman drew on himself more than on his imagination. "Well," he says when asked if this is the case, "let's just say that the progression of this character [Donald "Sully" Sullivan] goes from not being available to becoming available, and that's too close for comfort."

His time in Cleveland was one of conflict. Newman felt an obligation to his family, but he also hated the sporting goods business. "It was a marvelous shop," he said archly many years ago, "and sold all kinds of things—camping equipment, cameras, odd radio components.

There's no question that there can be great romance and exhilaration in retailing." But really, how are you going to keep them down in the shop after they've seen Williams Bay? Restless and bored, Paul worked at other jobs as well as at the store and pulled in a nice income. He managed a golf range and was able to find some outlet for his acting desires by doing some local radio. Television, then in its infancy, had come to Cleveland, and Paul was hired to do a live commercial for the National City Bank five nights a week during the 11 pm news broadcast. "I looked about four years old," he says, marveling. "How the hell they chose me, I don't know."

Allan Scott Newman was born later that year, but it was clear that Cleveland was not the place for Jackie and Paul to settle down in. Life had to be lived with more romance. In 1951 Newman's family sold the Newman-Stern Company and he was liberated. That September, he, Jackie, and Scott moved to New Haven, Connecticut, where he enrolled in a three-year program for a master's degree in directing at the Yale University School of Drama.

Newman has said repeatedly throughout his career that he willingly gave up a steady living in Shaker Heights to do this not because of any driving impulse to act and direct but rather simply to escape a life that he says "meant nothing" to him: "I knew that I was running away from merchandising." But he also admits that acting was "the only thing I ever approached doing very well in college." Probably both reasons influenced him. "I don't know that I was running toward the theater," he said at the end of 1994. "I was going to Yale as a safety net. I figured that I would try to make some kind of go at being an actor, or a director, really. And if I couldn't make it, I would have a master's degree and could teach."

Once he was faced with the demands of his studies, reality quickly overtook romance. He has said of his college acting that "I had no idea what I was doing. I learned my lines by rote and simply said them, without spontaneity, without any idea of dealing with the forces around me onstage, without knowing what it meant to think and react," but those are the words of someone who came to realize this only after long study and experience.

He did know from the outset that he was not an instinctive actor but rather one who had to "think" his way into a role. "I've always considered myself an emotional Republican," he says, acknowledging a Shaker Heights trait. "I'm not very good at revealing myself. I cover it up by telling terrible dirty jokes." And he adds, "I was terrorized by the emotional

RIGHT
With his chiseled features, Newman looked like a Greek god when he began as a Warner Bros. contract player. Many also thought he looked a lot like Marlon Brando.

requirements of being an actor. Acting is like letting your pants down; you're exposed." He was reminded of this shortly after arriving at Yale and accepting a part in Shaw's *Saint Joan* without first looking at what it demanded. When he got home to the boardinghouse where he and his wife and son lived, and looked at his lines, "the first thing I saw in the script was that my character was supposed to be weeping on stage. The muscles contracted in my stomach, and immediately I tried to figure out some way to play the whole thing facing upstage. And then I thought, 'What an ass. I drag my family with only $900 in the bank all the way to Connecticut and then think of ways I can cop out …' I took that script downstairs to the boiler room and said to myself, 'OK, Buddy, you are going to sit here until you find out where it is going to come from or you can get out of this business right now.'" Some years later he recalled, "That performance was probably as full and rich as anything I've done."

There is no surprise in learning that, despite his apprehensions, he did well in his first year at Yale. So well that when the term ended in June 1952 several instructors encouraged him to go to New York City for the summer and test his luck. If nothing worked out, he would return to Yale in the fall. He found an apartment for his family on Staten Island for $60 a month, sold encyclopedias to help with expenses (needing money while at Yale, he once sold $1,200 worth in ten days), and made the rounds to casting agents.

His luck was of course good. Newman's Luck is always good; to hear him tell it, the Luck Fairy practically lives at his house. Without much trouble he landed a couple of small television parts and a continuing role on a comedy called *The Aldrich Family*, which brought in $200 a month, and so he stayed on. In the early 1950s he had steady work on TV shows, among them the CBS public affairs series *You Are There*, which broadcast live re-creations of historical events. He portrayed Socrates, Aristotle, Julius Caesar and the American Revolutionary War patriot Nathan Hale.

Well, with looks like his, who was he supposed to play? In later life he has aged gracefully, and now his face has the finely etched look of someone on a postage stamp. But as a young man his face was something from an ancient coin. With his chiseled features he looked like a Greek god. To some people, such good looks could only be unnatural. Over the years there have been rumors that he has had plastic surgery or, perhaps more insidious, that he has special eyedrops flown in from Sweden to make his eyes bluer. Both, he says, are false.

Newman as the private detective Lew Harper, having just given his face a morning wake-up in a basin of ice water. This is something Newman does when he's had a bad night's sleep.

He does stick his face in a basin of ice water if he's had a bad night's sleep (we see him do this at the beginning of *Harper*, and in *The Sting*), but if that's all it took to look divine, the world would be full of Adonises. Newman's "luck" here is great genes, plus a daily sauna, countless sit-ups, and lots of exercise on bikes and weight machines.

His looks were something he had to grow into as an actor, as he learned when he went to Broadway in a play loaded with sexual yearning and attraction. At the end of 1952 he had about $250 in the bank and Jackie was pregnant with their second child when his money worries effectively ended for life. He landed the role of Alan Seymour, the ineffectual well-meaning rich boy who loses his girl to a physically magnetic friend in William Inge's Pulitzer Prize–winning drama *Picnic*. For $150 a week he was also the understudy for Ralph

Meeker, the lead who played the sexy, braggart stranger Hal Carter who strolls into the lives of two families with no men in them and changes the emotional landscape in a small Kansas town. The play, in which comfortable illusions prove no match for basic impulses, opened at the Music Box on 19 February 1953. Newman earned excellent notices as Alan and made the annual list of "promising personalities" in *Theater World*. He received a second mention from Brooks Atkinson of *The New York Times*, who wrote in a piece six months after the opening that the play was the best of the season, and added, "When *Picnic* was new did we all fully appreciate the taste and insight of Paul Newman's acting as Alan Seymour, the rich suitor? If not, let this stand as belated recognition." The play ran for fourteen months, and when Meeker took a vacation Newman filled in for him. Afterward he asked director Joshua Logan if he could play the part of Hal in the road company. Logan's response took him aback.

Newman's angry reponse to a critic who wrote that the problem with *Hud* is that he "has a face that doesn't look lived in" was, "That's exactly what made the bastard dangerous. The whole *point* of the character is that he has a face that doesn't look lived in."

"Well, it was a very interesting performance, but you don't carry any sexual threat at all," he said.

Although Newman says it took some time for him to get over the evaluation, he's come to conclude, "At that particular point, I probably didn't. That sort of thing has a lot to do with conviction." (He certainly got it later. Hud Bannon, whom he played in 1963's *Hud*, is the personification of sexual threat.)

Logan's advice was that he get into shape, and Newman says, "the way I translated that was six hours in the gym every day." Eventually he did take over the lead, having worked on both his muscles and his manner, and having learned that "You can measure each woman and find ways of being gallant, of listening, of crowding, of pursuing."

The understudy to *Picnic*'s two female leads was a twenty-three-year-old blonde with a languid Southern drawl and a steel-trap intellect, Joanne Woodward. The two had met earlier, in passing, in the agent John Foreman's office in New York. (Foreman and Newman would later become partners in a movie production company.) She had arrived on time for an appointment with Foreman, only to be kept waiting by a meeting between Foreman and Newman that ran late. Newman, dressed in his only suit, a conservative seersucker number, was, he says, "introduced to her by way of apology." She was unimpressed, judging him by his appearance to be a snotty college boy; nor was he bowled over. But thrown together in the cast of *Picnic* they soon became friends who over coffee could easily talk about plays and acting and the gossip of Broadway.

Paul's and Jackie's first daughter, Susan, was born during the run of the play. The Newmans were then living in a bedroom community on Long Island, a short commute from Manhattan, and Paul went back and forth every day. He has always been guarded about his personal life, especially his marriages, and all that is known is that the marriage to Jackie was under stress by then but that he was unwilling to end it.

Newman was also at this time accepted into the Actors Studio, run by Lee Strasberg. The Actors Studio was the temple of Method acting, a theory developed at the turn of the century by Konstantin Stanislavsky, the actor-director-producer who founded the Moscow Art Theater and staged some of the original productions of Chekhov and Gorky. The subordination of the actor to the playwright's vision, and his conscious emotional experience of his

OVERLEAF
At the Actors Studio c. 1953. "I just sat there and watched how people did things and had enough sense not to open my big mouth."

part, are cornerstones of the system. Admission to the studio came by successfully passing two auditions. At least it did for people with less luck than Newman. A woman friend had successfully managed the first and was invited back for the second, but her partner for the scene was out of town. She asked Paul to fill in. Whoever kept track of these things assumed that this was his second, too, and soon there was a letter telling him he had been accepted. Even though he believes that "during my audition they mistook terror—which is what I felt—for performed emotion," Newman didn't argue.

The Actors Studio was a zesty place to be in the mid-1950s. It was the garden in which post-war American acting flowered. Besides Strasberg, the teachers included Elia Kazan, who would direct Newman in the stage version of *Sweet Bird of Youth*, and Martin Ritt, who would direct him in six movies and become a close friend. Among his classmates were Marlon Brando, James Dean, Julie Harris, Karl Malden, Geraldine Page, Kim Stanley, Maureen Stapleton, Rod Steiger, Eli Wallach—and Joanne Woodward. In the midst of all this

The Warner Brothers: (left to right) Jack, Harry, and Albert, c. 1947. Their studio was a pioneer in sound films and produced *The Jazz Singer,* the first talkie.

talent Newman considered himself an "untuned piano" who needed a lot of tinkering. "It was monkey see, monkey do," he says. "Man, I just sat back there and watched how people did things and had enough sense not to open my big mouth." Outside the studio, however, he was friendly with his classmates. Kim Stanley had one of the female leads in *Picnic*. He would later act on Broadway with Karl Malden in *The Desperate Hours* and with Geraldine Page in both the stage and film versions of *Sweet Bird of Youth*. He hardly knew Brando or Dean, even though he would frustratingly spend the next few years being mistaken for one or the other. Rudy Bond, another classmate, recalls walking down the street with Newman in the early 1950s and trying to make him be realistic about his future.

"I don't think you've got a chance in this business because you look like Marlon," he said. "Who's going to hire you?"

Almost everyone. Movie studios had noticed him for his looks and his talent and had made offers. He worried about being swallowed by Hollywood's insatiable hunger for new talent and turned down the first ones. He found the people brash and uncouth and the total loss of independence that a contract entailed to be worrisome. But, he finally reasoned, how many times could one rebuff offers before they stopped altogether? And so he accepted an offer from Warner Bros. for a five-year contract beginning at $1,000 a week. When *Picnic* closed in the spring of 1954, rather than go out with the road company as he had planned he went to Los Angeles, leaving his family behind while he assessed the situation.

The standard studio contract he signed with Warner Bros. Pictures, Inc. on 8 April 1954 granted almost all the latitude afforded by a seventeenth-century indentured servant agreement, although it *did* pay better. He would receive raises of $250 a week for each of the next four years. The fifth year would bring a raise of $500, from $2,000 to $2,500. He was guaranteed two movies with a minimum of ten weeks' pay and with an option on a third, and would be given at least feature billing on the screen, in advertising and in publicity.

In return, Newman gave up everything but his shadow. Apart from appearing in whatever movie they assigned him, Newman granted Warner Bros. "all rights, including the use of the artist's name, voice, likeness, acts, poses, plays, appearances, etc.," although there was a provision for him to go to New York each year for not more than nine months to appear in what the contract called a "first-class stage presentation." The contract would be suspended for the period he was gone and that time added on before renewal.

He was barely there before he wondered what he was doing. Executive Sam Spiegel, who had once changed his name to S. P. Eagle, tried to persuade Newman to improve his name to something more "American," or more precisely, less Jewish. Newman would have none of it. When Spiegel then tried to tell him that Newman was not very phonetic, he shrugged and said, very well, he'd change it to S. P. Newman.

After the question of his name was resolved came the question of what his first movie would be. Considering the answer, only Newman's Luck can serve to explain why there was even a second.

Warner Bros. had signed another up-and-coming actor besides Newman, and

director Elia Kazan had narrowed down the choice of the young male lead for

his next picture to the two of them. In the end he decided, on the basis of their

Newman's Own

screen tests, that the part of Cal Trask in the movie adaptation of John

Steinbeck's East of Eden *would go to James Dean. Second prize was*

nearly a one-way ticket out of town. Newman was assigned to

The Silver Chalice, *a religious costume extravaganza based*

on Thomas B. Costain's novel about the Holy Grail,

produced and directed by Victor Saville. Both were shot at

the same time on the Warner lot.

LEFT

**In *Hud* (1963). After Newman filled
in for the vacationing lead in *Picnic*
on Broadway in 1953, he asked
director Josh Logan if he could play
the part in the road company. Logan ·
responded, "You don't carry any sexual
threat at all." Ten years later, as Hud
Bannon, he was the personification
of sexual threat.**

RIGHT

**Newman has the capacity to look
drop-dead handsome or tough with
an underlay of vulnerability, or both
at once.**

It is hard to imagine two more polar screen debuts. Dean rode a rocket to stardom as he defined misunderstood youth. Newman was wrapped in a cocoon of Warnercolor and Cinemascope, stuck in a time capsule, and sent back 2,000 years. To make things even worse, he was cast opposite Pier Angeli, Dean's great love. As it would turn out, at almost every turn over the next few years, Dean, one way or another, would directly affect Newman's career. Joanne Woodward also tested for *East of Eden*, and the sexually tense scene with Dean in which she plays a puzzled, earnest girl trying to understand good from bad is a powerful teaser of what might have been.

Although he did not know him well, Newman was a great admirer of Dean, even envied him his ability to grasp a part. He felt the same way about Brando and Kim Stanley and Geraldine Page and Eli Wallach and Anne Jackson, "almost any of the people that I know that were instinctive actors. It's the same way a technician admires John McEnroe."

Warner Bros. has a screen test that the two took together in May 1954 that is interesting not only for its own sake but for the pleasure the pair seemed to have in making it. Newman is dressed in a light shirt and bow tie and looks like Ohio; Dean's shirt is dark and open-necked, and there is a sense of wildness about him. They stand side by side. A voice offscreen, presumably Kazan's, says, "Go ahead, you queens."

The pair laugh and Newman says rapidly, "What? What? What? What?" They are instructed to show their profiles, then turn back to full face. Newman's is oval, Dean's is like an inverted triangle, his long hair combed up, his cheeks narrowing to a flat jaw. Each is magnetic. Both are young midwesterners trying to sound worldly. Either would have made a fine Cal Trask. But in movies, image and looks are almost everything and Dean, who grew up in a small Indiana town, had more the aura of someone from a rural family than Newman, who still had not shed his suburban past.

"Do you think you can hit the bobby sox league?" Dean is asked.

"Depends on how many want to go," he answers with a cool grin while flipping a pocket knife in his right hand.

"Do you think the girls will go for Paul, Jim?"

Before he can respond, Newman says in a tough-guy voice, "It's a point of whether I go for the girls." They both laugh.

Newman wearing what he called his "cocktail dress," and looking a lot like Brando, in *The Silver Chalice* (1954), his first picture. Later he took out an ad in the *Los Angeles Times,* apologizing for the film and urging people not to watch it on television.

"Paul, do you think the girls will go for Jim?"

"Oh, *great*," he says with almost a giggle, but meaning it.

Dean looks at Newman. "Kiss me," he says solemnly.

"Can't here," Newman tells him without missing a beat, then they both dissolve in laughter.

For all their bonhomie in the screen test, Newman and Dean scarcely knew each other despite what has become the common assumption, that they spent a lot of time together in Los Angeles. The same is true of his relationship with Brando. Newman says that the reports over the years "that Brando and Dean and I were great friends simply are not true. I've probably spoken to Marlon twelve times in forty years, and I saw Jimmy briefly at the studio and a couple of times when he was out in California, shooting *East of Eden*, but certainly there was no great friendship there. Both of them were something less than acquaintances."

Newman grew to wish that he could have been less acquainted with *The Silver Chalice*. He played Basil, the Greek slave who was the sculptor of the silver chalice used at the Last Supper. Clad in a short toga—"a cocktail dress" was his description—Newman was so

LEFT
**Director Elia Kazan with
some of Newman's finest
contemporaries in the
early '50s: Marlon Brando
(looking rather like
Newman), Julie Harris,
and James Dean, probably
around the time** *East of
Eden* **was filmed in 1954.**

ABOVE
**A portrait of the artist as a young
man,** *c.* **1954, whom Warner Bros. had
no idea how to use to their, or his,
advantage.**

conscious of what he felt were his bony legs that, as he said with some glee years later, he refused to look at the camera. With such lines to deliver as, "Helena, is it really you? What a joy!" it is no wonder. He was appalled by the outcome, but no more so than many critics, who panned both him and the movie (which went on to gross what was in those days a very successful $4,500,000). A. H. Weiler in *The New York Times* wrote that Newman "bears a striking resemblance to Marlon Brando but his contribution is hardly outstanding. As a youth who has been cheated of his rich inheritance by his covetous uncle, sold into slavery and eventually chosen to recreate the Holy Relic, he is given mainly to thoughtful posing and automatic speechmaking. And despite the fact that he is desired by the extremely fetching Helena [Virginia Mayo] and the wistful Deborra [Pier Angeli], his wife, he is rarely better than wooden in his reaction to these fairly spectacular damsels." John McCarter in *The New Yorker* was more succinct: "Newman delivered his lines with the emotional fervor of a Putnam Division conductor announcing local stops."

Newman was "horrified, traumatized" when he saw *The Silver Chalice* for the first time. He was also, he says, drunk. *The Desperate Hours* was in tryouts in Philadelphia in preparation for Broadway, and a friend had come from New York to see him in the show. Afterwards, several others joined them and they went to an all-night movie house to see the movie. Newman is an aficionado of beer and of homemade popcorn, and his practice of taking one or both into a theater was already commonplace for him. This evening was no exception. "We must have smuggled four cases of beer into that place," he says. "And we finished them all. This friend of mine, who had just recovered from hepatitis, couldn't drink. They had a musical going on [after the movie] and he wanted to see it, so he stayed. [The rest of us] got half-way down the block when another guy realized he had left his gloves in the theater. So we went back. The usher shoved his light underneath the seats. There was [my friend] sitting in the middle of four cases of empty beer cans." Newman and his friends could only laugh. "He became a legend as a result," he said recently.

In 1963, just before the movie began a week-long run on television in Los Angeles, he paid $1,200 for a large black-bordered ad in the *Los Angeles Times* that read, "Paul Newman apologizes every night this week." To his chagrin, all that did was make thousands more people tune in to see what he was so sorry about. "A classic example of the arrogance of the affluent," he said a few years later. (An often-reported story is that, around 1980, Newman screened *The Silver Chalice* at home in Connecticut for some friends. Each was given a metal pot and a wooden spoon but this was a demon not easily exorcized. "It was fun for about the first reel," he said later, "and then the awfulness of the thing took over." The events are correct, he says, but the movie was Ronald Reagan's *Bedtime for Bonzo*.)

"I feel that I didn't quite come up to my expectations," he said of *The Silver Chalice*, with some understatement, in *The New York Times* a couple of years after its release. "It did one thing for me, though. It enabled me to vow that I'd never make another costume picture. They're for actors like Robert Taylor, not for me." He also learned, he says, that "if you want to survive, you have to show your ass. You can't walk in and play it safe."

The Silver Chalice was Newman's first real theatrical failure, and in retrospect the damage he suffered seems more psychological than actual—which can be just as crippling. To overcome what he saw as a disaster, and fearful of what it could do to his nascent career, he quickly took advantage of the clause in his contract that allowed him to do plays and returned to Broadway before Warner Bros. could assign him to another movie or loan him to another studio. On 10 February 1955 he opened in Joseph Hayes's melodrama *The Desperate Hours* at the Ethel Barrymore Theater, directed by Robert Montgomery. This time he didn't play it safe. In a part that would be portrayed on the screen by Humphrey Bogart, Newman played Glenn Griffin, a psychotic killer and the leader of three escaped convicts who take refuge in the home of a respectable, law-abiding family while they wait for one of their confederates to send them a package of escape money. Newman's Actors Studio classmate Karl Malden played Dan Hilliard, the father. Brooks Atkinson called the play a "literate thriller ... told with pace, economy and precision ... [that] shatters the

Newman as the psychotic killer Glenn Griffin in the Broadway production of *The Desperate Hours* (1955), with Karl Malden and Nancy Coleman.

nerves." He praised Hayes as a "genuine writer … interested in the inner life of his people" and said that "Paul Newman plays the boss thug with a wildness that one is inclined to respect." (By way of introduction Atkinson wrote: "It is a cops-and-jailbirds yarn by Joseph Hayes, who wrote it first in the shape of a taut novel. It is also a movie, though not to be released until next year; and a decade from now it will be a musical drama with a brassy orchestration and a symbolic ballet.")

New York was then the center of television, and stage actors were perfect for the medium because the performances were live and the same as doing a stage show, only to a vast but invisible audience. Newman was much in demand. He did a couple of episodes of a CBS show called *Appointment with Adventure*, joined Eva Marie Saint and Frank Sinatra in a musical version of Thornton Wilder's *Our Town* for *Producer's Showcase* on NBC, and starred in the *Philco Television Playhouse* production on that network of *The Death of Billy the Kid*, written by Gore Vidal, who became a good friend of Newman and Joanne Woodward. Newman also starred in the 1958 movie adaptation, *The Left-Handed Gun*.

The period is looked back on as the golden age of television, and in 1956 Newman appeared on the *U. S. Steel Hour* in an adaptation of Mark Harris's novel *Bang the Drum Slowly*. Along with *Marty* this is one of the most highly regarded productions of the time.

It tells the story of a dim-witted, second-string baseball catcher determined to conceal his cancer from the team, and who entrusts his secret only to Henry Wiggen, a star pitcher played by Newman. In the book the action takes place in ball parks and hotels all over the country, but in a wonderful act of compression it was done for TV live, on a single sound stage, all in forty-eight minutes. Time had to be built in between the scenes for actors to move from one set to the next in the blackout. One way to do that when a commercial wasn't necessary was to spotlight the narrator, Newman's character, who took the audience through a retrospective account of his friend's life and death.

"There's not much room in the studio here," he told the audience at the beginning of the production. "You have to use your imagination."

That seductive little phrase captures the magic of live television. It made the immediacy one feels in a theater felt in a million living rooms and subjected the actors to all the pitfalls of an unstoppable performance.

"Once, in a military drama, when I had to salute another officer ... I had my fly unzipped," Newman recalled some years ago. "My shirttail was sticking out—just the shirttail, fortunately. But despite their perils, television dramas were exciting and vibrant in those days because they were live. ... The trouble was ... what could have been good Broadway plays were burned out in a single night on *Robert Montgomery Presents*, *The Philco Playhouse*, *Studio One* and the rest of them. That whole glorious period of television disappeared and nothing has come along to replace it."

What has happened instead, he says, is that television's "huge appetite has accelerated the exhaustion of talent and the exhaustion of imagination. And coupled with that, of course, was the need to sell product and design things for the lowest common denominator, and the lowest common denominator kept dropping and dropping until," he adds with a laugh, "you really don't know where the lowest common denominator is now."

He had earlier played a less type-cast athlete than a young baseball player. In an effort to extend his range, Newman, then thirty, took the part of a washed-up, fifty-five-year-old punch-drunk fighter in the TV adaptation of Hemingway's short story *The Battler*, which was shown on NBC's *Playwright's '56* in October 1955. The part was originally to be played by James Dean with Newman as Nick Adams, the narrator who meets the old pug and tells the story. Newman had looked forward to working with Dean, but Dean's death on 30 September at the age of twenty-four, when he crashed the Porsche he was driving down a highway at more than 100 mph, made him want nothing to do with the project because, he says, "I didn't want to gain anything as a result of someone else's tragedy." The show was so close to presentation, however, that a few days later the director begged Newman to reconsider because they couldn't find a suitable replacement at such short notice.

Newman was not the only ambivalent one connected with the show. A. E. Hotchner, the author of the teleplay and a Hemingway biographer, wrote to Hemingway that "we were forced to fill the part by risking young Newman in the lead." Some risks are well taken. Newman did very well, and Hotchner has become one of his closest friends as well as his partner in the wildly successful Newman's Own line. (In 1962 Newman played the part again, this time in a Twentieth Century–Fox movie called *Adventures of a Young Man*, because he wanted to see what he had learned about acting in the interim. He was disappointed.

"I tried to do what I did in the TV show," he said, "and that wasn't the way to go at it.") His assured performance as the Battler in the television show impressed director Robert Wise and producer Charles Schnee, who themselves were looking for a replacement for James Dean for another project. They asked MGM to take Newman on a loan-out from Warner Bros. to play the former middleweight boxing champion Rocky Graziano in *Somebody Up There Likes Me*.

At this time Newman would spend weeks preparing for a part, trying to find out as much as possible about his character so he could get inside its skin. "The actor's got to come to the part; the part doesn't come to the actor," he said, and he approached the role of Graziano with characteristic thoroughness, logging innumerable hours in the gym to build a boxer's body. He also worked hard at learning boxing technique, and even sparred with professionals.

On top of that, "I almost *lived* with Graziano for two weeks. I'd meet him at ten in the morning and wouldn't leave him until four the next morning. We went down to his old neighborhood, went up to Stillman's Gymnasium [on West 54th Street, the inner sanctum of the sport at the time]. But I could see that he didn't want to talk about his family. So one night at the Embers, Bob Wise … and I tried to get Rocky stoned so that he'd loosen up and talk about himself. The fact is, Rocky loosened *us* up. We told him *our* life histories. He poured us into two taxicabs. … I never really did absorb the character, though I certainly sponged a lot. I wound up being a Graziano rather than *the* Graziano."

Newman was in something of an impossible situation at this point in his career. He was getting roles meant for Dean, whose stature in death rose to sanctified heights, and he was constantly being unfavorably compared either to Dean or to Brando or to both. For instance, Newman's work in *Somebody Up There Likes Me* was highly applauded, yet many critics then diluted that praise by declaring that Newman's use of shuffling body language and a mouthful of marbles, deez-and-dem voice, was ersatz Brando. "Mr. Newman

"The actor's got to come to the part, the part doesn't come to the actor," Newman has said. He came to the part of Rocky Graziano by logging innumerable hours in the gym and sparring with professionals to make *Somebody Up There Likes Me* as realistic as possible.

... plays the role of Graziano well, making the pug and Marlon Brando almost indistinguishable," went one review. But years later Newman learned in a conversation with Graziano that the question really was, who was imitating whom?

"[Graziano] told me, in the way only he could," Newman recalled. "'I was sparrin' around, really workin' hard, and there was this funny, strange kid standin' here. He'd sit down and *watch*, you know? Finally, I sez, "What are you doin' here, kid?" He sez, "Well, I'd like you to come and see a show of mine." I sez, "What do you mean, a stage show? I don't want to see no fuckin' stage show! Why'd I wanna see a fuckin' stage show for?"' This is Rocky talking, you know; I think that's where *my* terrible vocabulary came from. So Rocky said, 'Well, kid, do you sing or sumpin?' He sez, "No." I figured the kid was a spear carrier or sumpin'. Anyway, the kid gives me two tickets, and when I tell my wife, she sez, "Oh, that's a pretty good play." So we go see the play, and it's a thing about a streetcar, written by this famous author, what*ever* it was. And I see this kid onstage. So I sez, "This kid is playin' *me*!"'

"Well, so much for the Brando comparison. Turns out, we both had the same model. Marlon did his earlier in *A Streetcar Named Desire*, which had already been on the screen by the time I played Rocky. So, in a way, the reviews were accurate."

In a joke told at the time, a kid walks up to Newman and asks him for his autograph. Newman gives it.

"Oh, *Paul Newman*," he says, a little surprised. Then after a short pause he asks, "Can I have another?"

"OK," Newman says, and signs again. Just as the boy starts to walk away, Newman calls out, "Wait, what do you want with two?"

"I can trade them for a Marlon Brando," he answers with a shrug.

There were more serious problems that Newman had to face at this time besides whether he was doing Marlon Brando or Jimmy Dean impersonations. For all the success in his career, his marriage to Jackie had continued to deteriorate. Their second daughter, Stephanie, was born in 1955, and he was now the father of three small children, towards whom he felt an enormous responsibility. Exacerbating an already difficult marriage was what seems the almost unavoidable development of his relationship with Joanne Woodward. The values of his childhood made him recoil at the idea of divorce and the inevitable

problems it brings, especially to children. Moreover, Woodward knew these problems first-hand from her parents' divorce, which entailed long separations from her father (a vice president of the publisher Scribner's). So they agreed not to see each other again.

Newman found temporary refuge from the turmoil in drinking, a leaky shelter at best. In July 1956, just after the completion of *Somebody Up There Likes Me*, he was arrested when police charged him with driving his new Volkswagen through shrubbery outside the Jolly Fisherman restaurant on Main St. in Roslyn, Long Island, not far from his home in Fresh Meadows. He says that after leaving the restaurant he dented a fire hydrant and then ran a red light. When the police, who had been called after the incident at the restaurant, pulled him over, Newman compounded his problem by telling them, "I'm acting for Rocky Graziano. What do you want?"

Officer Rocco (Rocky) Caggiano replied, "I'm Rocky, too, and you're under arrest for leaving the scene of an accident."

Newman, wearing a suit and tie, was taken into the station, his left wrist handcuffed to the right one of a beefy cop. It made quite a picture in the New York *Daily News* the next

day. Newman's Luck was for once nowhere to be found, for the station happened to be full of newspaper photographers and reporters who were awaiting developments in a local kidnapping and who were all too happy to get photos and details of a movie star's problems while they waited.

Motion pictures are not always released in the order in which they are made. Before filming *Somebody Up There Likes Me*, Newman had gained the lead of yet another picture in which the original star was suddenly unavailable. In this case Glenn Ford dropped out of *The Rack* and in October 1955 Warner Bros. loaned out Newman to Loew's at his

salary of $1,250 a week to play an American Army officer on trial for collaborating with the enemy during the Korean War. In flashbacks the audience relives the tortures inflicted on Capt. Edward W. Hall Jr., and sees him finally succumb to pain and brainwashing. The movie, adapted by Stewart Stern from a teleplay by Rod Serling, very much reflects the time when it was made and has not held up all that well. Still, it displays Newman's combination of vulnerability and toughness. Here was a hero at once a loner and alienated but also emotionally exposed. In particular, the scenes between Walter Pidgeon as the father and Newman as his namesake powerfully reveal their broken relationship.

While he filmed *The Rack*, Warner Bros. made another deal to keep their property busy. In December 1955 they signed an additional agreement with Loew's, this one for *Somebody Up There Likes Me*. The price would be the same, $1,250 a week. To ensure maximum use of Newman, Warner Bros. agreed to instruct him "to report the day following completion of all services required of him by you in connection with *The Rack* for costume fitting, publicity, etc." There would be no charge for his services until the movie began filming. But he was also guaranteed to be sent to New York first class on 23 December so that he could be with his family for Christmas.

The Rack was scheduled to be released during the filming of *Somebody Up There Likes Me*. That idea was scrapped after only a few premières because once shooting was underway and the studio executives glimpsed what the finished movie could be, they were certain that *Somebody Up There Likes Me* was going to be a huge success. They hoped to parlay that success into a double winner by postponing the wide release of *The Rack* in the hope that it could be carried on Newman's shirttails or, perhaps more aptly, boxing trunks. Newman was in great physical form after his months of training, and the studio thought they had a rare hybrid: a sex symbol who could also act.

They were right in that *Somebody Up There Likes Me* was a hit, and they were right in that their sex symbol could certainly act. But right doesn't necessarily make box-office might, and not even great reviews could help *The Rack*. *The New York Times'* movie critic, Bosley Crowther, called Newman's "brilliantly detailed performance" of a man in moral torment "a remarkable tour de force. In his facial expressions, his gestures, his pauses and his use of his voice, he makes apparent in one figure a singularly personal tragedy." Even so, the movie came and went without much stir, although Newman's notices were another addition to his rising reputation as an actor. Newman thinks that the movie was worthwhile but is less impressed with his performance in *The Rack*. It "really aspired to something," he says,

Newman's ability to combine toughness with vulnerability came through in his portrayal in *The Rack* (1956) of Capt. Edward W. Hall Jr., an American serviceman brainwashed by his captors and then court-martialed after his release.

"and nobody went to see it. A fine example of me trying too hard."

This portion of his career is a fine example, as well, of a studio using rather than nurturing an actor. As evidenced in Warner Bros. ordering Newman to report for work on *Somebody Up There Likes Me* the day after finishing *The Rack*, the studio's greatest concern was that a money-producing actor work as much as possible, with no particular view to his long-term professional life. So far as Warner Bros. was concerned, actors come and go but movies have to be turned out at a regular pace. Newman was hardly singled out for this treatment; this was the life of a contract player. If Newman's varied roles served to make him a bright star, all the better. If they simply burned him up, well, there were more where he came from. So Warner Bros. took what for them was the obvious course and tried to make Newman into a conventional movie hero. Which would prove to be a mistake.

He worked almost constantly during this time. In 1957 he starred in *Until They Sail*, a wartime romance based on James Michener's *Return to Paradise*, for which he was paid the $1,500 a week his contract called for, and for which Warner Bros. received $2,500 a week for his loan-out to MGM. Immediately before that he had made *The Helen Morgan Story*, in which Warner Bros. finally got around to using him rather than loaning him out to another studio. Newman is Larry Maddux, a Prohibition-era gangster who seduces and then exploits the alcoholic cabaret singer Helen Morgan, played by Ann Blyth. The movie had been in the works for many years; at least forty actresses tested for the part. In 1950 it was announced that Doris Day would do the role; Peggy Lee and Patty Page were also mentioned at various other times.

The movie was called *Both Ends of the Candle* abroad, but by any name the finished product was nothing particularly special; Newman's one-word description is "Uggghhh." Even so, the force of his *Desperate Hours* hoodlum comes through vividly. James Powers wrote in *Variety*, "Paul Newman is excellent as the gangster—so good, in fact, that the picture seems to be about him rather than Helen Morgan." And the Hollywood Foreign Press Association gave him a Golden Globe as one of the most promising newcomers of the year.

There was a strong pattern emerging here, which was that regardless of the merit of the finished movie Newman could be banked on for a solid performance, whether it was of a brainwashed young American soldier, a venal gangster, or a tough boxer whose capable fists seem destined to win him only a life in prison but who instead fights his way to a world championship and respectability.

Newman's rise coincided with the emergence of a new kind of movie hero, less predictable and more inclined to ambiguity. The male stars when Newman came to Hollywood were tough guys such as Humphrey Bogart and Robert Mitchum; swashbucklers such as Errol Flynn and Clark Gable; strong, silent types such as Gary Cooper; handsome guys of dignity such as William Holden; fatherly types such as Spencer Tracy and Walter Pidgeon; and one-of-a-kinds such as Cary Grant and John Wayne. For all their success, they were ageing and the public was looking for new faces, but the studios, unsure of how to meet the challenge of television, publicly pretended there was no challenge and, seemingly para-lysed, did almost nothing to develop new stars to replace them. The four who did emerge in the 1950s—James Dean, Montgomery Clift, Marlon Brando and Newman—all came from Broadway, seldom the case today. The careers of the first three began explosively. They were given parts such as Cal Trask or Stanley Kowalski that were more intricate and held more promise of spectacular success than those given to Newman. But then Dean died in 1955 even before *Giant,* his third movie, was completed; Clift died in 1966. Brando was a supernova who self-destructed. Newman feels that Brando's image was one he has never matched, the sense of an "animal … the true grizzly. I never projected that. … It's a tough image to sustain—that you're an animal who has the ability to park in front of a whore-house without ever getting a parking ticket. … But Marlon also dared as an actor. It wasn't just image. And his rebellion came out of a true eccentricity, I think, and not as a rebellion for the sake of rebellion nor for the sake of image. I am sorry that he wasn't as disciplined as he was eccentric in his personal life."

Newman was the tortoise to their hares, although "terrier" is the word he tends to use: "I always see them as dogs that are trying to handle bones that are much too big for them, trying to dig up bones under fences when the fences are too deeply embedded. I am lucky to a fault, but I am also very determined. I will somehow *get* that bone."

Whichever the animal, his tenacity served him well. Newman has never had the kind of defining role that Dean had in, say, *Rebel Without a Cause*, or Brando had in *On the Waterfront*. Initially, those two bode well to be the dominant stars of their generation. Even so, Newman was a contender; and now, in terms of a lifetime of work relying less on pyrotechnics than simply living a part, he has eclipsed them.

Where Newman differed most from Brando and Dean and Clift is that he looked like one thing—a breathtakingly handsome hero—but was really a more complex, less easily cate-gorized actor. The others were pretty much what they played, which is not to detract from them but to suggest that their type-casting served them well. It was out of order for Newman. His best roles have come where he has had the opportunity to go against his ob-vious looks and play flawed men whose humanity is the counterbalance to his flawless appearance. Paul Newman as a total hero is too good to be true; no one can be so handsome and capable without either stirring resentment or appearing two-dimensional. This kind of thinking, however, was not endemic to the studio mentality, and it is as good a reason as any to explain why Newman didn't really come into his own until after he extracted himself in 1959 from the binds of being a contract player.

What Newman and these other young men shared beside talent at the outset of their careers was a determined, sometimes eccentric independence that put them at odds with a system that had heretofore treated its stars like plantation workers, ordered to do what the studio bosses told them, from how to dress to where to live and with whom to be seen.

In return, especially in the '30s and '40s, when the studios had what might be called an economic understanding with the Los Angeles district attorney's office and many top police officials, the stars were shielded from the unpleasantness of being arrested for, as Lloyd Shearer, a long-time Hollywood observer, so nicely put it, "such peccadilloes as homosexuality, transvestitism, drunken driving, assault and battery, drug-addiction, disorderly conduct, non-payment of alimony, fraud and contributing to the delinquency of a minor." Yet worse even than the commission of any of the foregoing was involvement with politics. Bad acts could be covered up. Political acts, such as publicly supporting lettuce pickers or advocating freedom of speech before the House Committee on Un-American Activities, as Humphrey Bogart did in the '30s and '40s, was tantamount to corporate sacrilege, and with Bogart, in the end, Jack Warner prevailed even over the number one box-office draw of the day. The star's role was to be a screen fantasy whose supposed life was actually scripted for fan magazines, not a real person with opinions and commitments. Dean, Clift, Brando, and perhaps especially Newman—who has been particularly public in his political views— wanted none of that.

"I've discovered that in order to be a gold-plated success in this town it's almost mandatory that an actor open his private life to public view, get himself trapped into making more and more money and become a yes-man to Hollywood," he said after *The Helen Morgan Story* opened, in a story sub-headlined, "At Last He's Himself, Not Brando or Dean." "As of now, I've managed to avoid these problems. I keep my family life to myself, for the most part. I try to live quietly on a comfortable income and enjoy my work. I refuse to buy that big house and thus get trapped into making that fifth picture a year. Of course, by this time next year, I may forget all this. After all, it's pretty easy to become enamored of a Mercedes-Benz. But now I feel that enjoying life and work is much more important than vying for material success."

Judging from the way Newman has dressed for much of his life, one would think he had achieved little material success. For most of his early career, he had only one suit. Even today, his standard wear leans heavily towards jeans or khakis, a T-shirt, and loafers or running shoes. Sweat clothes are favored, too. For quite a while, a beer-can opener hung on a string around his neck. If for no other reason, the advent of pop-top cans got rid of that. On the third finger of his right hand is a nearly inch-square diamond-studded racing-award ring. Yet that casual-attired, race car–driver look is only his exterior. Inside is the poet and the lover of Bach who has strong opinions about which Glenn Gould recording is best.

By the end of 1956 it became even harder for Newman to keep his family life to himself, because Twentieth Century-Fox cast Paul and Joanne Woodward in *The Long, Hot Summer*, based on William Faulkner's novel *The Hamlet* and several of his short stories. It marked both the first of their acting collaborations and the end of his marriage. It was Jackie who halted the trauma by asking Paul for a divorce, which was accomplished in Mexico in 1957 with a minimum of fuss and publicity and with no evident rancor that could turn into a tug-of-war for the children's emotions. It was agreed that Scott, Susan, and Stephanie would live with their mother but have weekends and summers with their father. Relations between Paul and Jackie apparently remained cordial.

"The kids will never completely lose the scars of the divorce," he said a few years later, "but we're doing what we can to heal them."

Newman greatly values the benefit of letting parts of a character seep in by a kind of osmosis. Although he does it less now, for much of his career he would go to the movie locale some time ahead of the rest of the company to observe the people and their mannerisms so that he could add texture to his performance by picking up a piece or two of authentic business. For instance, he spent ten days living in a bunkhouse in Texas before *Hud* (1963), and two weeks in Mexico before making *The Outrage* (1964). Before *Hombre* (1967), in which he plays a white man raised by Apaches, Newman spent several days on an Indian reservation.

There he saw a man leaning against a building, his foot tucked up behind him on the doorstep. When Newman came back an hour later he noticed the man had not moved, and that stillness is a central part of his character.

"I stole the character of *Harper* from Bobby Kennedy," he said not long before Kennedy was assassinated. "The way Bobby listens … is very peculiar; there's an odd quality about it. He seems almost inattentive. If you didn't watch him closely, you'd think he wasn't listening. It's not that there isn't contact; he's really honed in and sharp. But it's not just listening, it's mulling and evaluating; while you're talking, you can see him preparing his rebuttal. It kind of puts you off until you get used to it. I thought it was a nice bit of business for a private detective."

Rehearsal, too, is important to him; he usually gives the studio two weeks' rehearsal time without pay because it "gives me a chance not to sit and intellectualize about a part but to get up on my feet and run through it, the same as I used to do for television shows. For television rehearsals they used to put a little tape on the floor and say, 'That's a wall,' and they put four chairs together and said, 'That's a bed,' and you followed those outlines without resorting to too much intellectualizing. This kind of experience has helped give a certain solidarity to what I finally do when the cameras start rolling. If you can rehearse a dozen key scenes with the other actors and get the style and the progression of the character, you've got the part licked."

For *The Long, Hot Summer* he went to Clinton, Missouri (which in the movie looks remarkably like Faulkner's home town of Oxford, Mississippi), in 1957 to absorb the son-of-the-South quality of the patrons of the pool halls, bars, and other local hangouts. He knew he had made friends after some of the men he'd been drinking with and studying took aside a reporter eager to explore the Newman-Woodward romance and suggested he leave town.

It was the kind of action that his character, Ben Quick—a roughneck who at the start of the picture is run out of town because of his perceived inclination to burn barns to settle grievances—would have applauded. Resettled in a place called Frenchman's Bend, Quick quickly ingratiates himself with Varner (Orson Welles), a man as greedy as he is tyrannical. There is a scornful, virginal daughter named Cara (Woodward), whom against her better judgment he arouses, and a weakling son, Jody (Anthony Franciosa), whom he does his best

INSET
The Long, Hot Summer (1958) was the first of eleven films that Newman and Joanne Woodward have made together. He has also directed her in four other films, plus one for television.

MAIN PICTURE
During read-throughs of *The Long, Hot Summer.* Joanne Woodward is to Newman's left and Anthony Franciosa next to her. Across the table are Lee Remick and Orson Welles.

to bully. Varner encourages and relishes it all. If this sounds a lot like Tennessee Williams and *Cat on a Hot Tin Roof*, which Newman would make a few months later, it is. Newman was voted "Outstanding Actor of the Year" at the Cannes Film Festival in May 1958 for his portrayal of Ben, and American critics were equally laudatory.

"Paul Newman is best as the roughneck who moves in with a thinly veiled sneer to knock down the younger generation and make himself the inheritor of the old man," Bosley Crowther wrote in *The New York Times*. "He has within his plowhand figure and behind his hard blue eyes the deep ugly deceptions of a neo-Huey Long. He could, if the script would let him, develop a classic character." (Thirty years later, in *Blaze*, Newman would play Governor Earl Long, the brother of the Louisiana demagogue.)

After *The Long, Hot Summer* he immediately began shooting *The Left-Handed Gun*, the story of Billy the Kid told as a Greek tragedy with modern analytic overtones. Newman had already acted in Gore Vidal's version on television, and for the movie he would not only receive his salary but for the first time would be among those sharing the profits. He owned 14⅙ percent, the production company 19⅙ percent, and Warner Bros. had the rest. A year before filming began Newman signed a deal with the producers that if they would give Arthur Penn, the director, not less than 2⅓ percent of the profits, then he would assign 1⅙ percent of his profits back to them "in order to induce you to enter into a contract with" the director. They did.

"I gave up some of my points?" Newman asked recently. "Well, Arthur didn't have any [and] he was the director. He ought to have points. He wanted to do [the movie]. My giving points wasn't an inducement, it was just that I thought he ought to have some interest in the movie."

The screenplay was originally titled *The Saga of Billy the Kid*, and it was a picture Newman had wanted to make for some time. The problem was, Warner Bros. kept stalling because they wanted it to have a happy ending. Newman was incredulous. "That's like filming the life of Abraham Lincoln," he said, "and … having his wife come in and say, 'Abe, dear, I forgot the tickets for the theater tonight. We'll have to stay home.'"

One of the problems for Warner Bros. was that in Vidal's original version Billy was rampantly homosexual, and while homosexuality was an underlying theme in the work of both

Vidal and Tennessee Williams, when it came to making *The Left-Handed Gun* and *Cat on a Hot Tin Roof*, no Hollywood studio was going to risk offending a generally homophobic nation of theatergoers. In the 1970s Newman hoped to do a movie called *The Front Runner*, about a homosexual track coach and one of his athletes, but, he says, "We could never get the script right, though we must have rewritten it five times. ... [It would have been a departure for me] as an actor, but not in terms of philosophy. I'm a supporter of gay rights. And not a closet supporter, either. From the time I was a kid, I never have been able to understand attacks on the gay community."

But in 1950s Hollywood Billy the Kid's character was better defined in terms of father-son relations than sexual preference. In Leslie Stevens's adaptation, shot in black and white, Billy is a character half boy, half man who has never known kindness until he is given a job by rancher John Tunstall (Colin Keith-Johnston), who has earned the hatred of the other ranchers in the New Mexico Territory by cutting the price of beef he sells to the Army. Billy comes to regard Tunstall as a father figure after the latter treats the young man with understanding.

Newman played a character half man and half boy in *The Left-Handed Gun*. One of his strengths was his ability to shift his face and manner in a moment from guile to murderous intent to a smile of dazzling innocence.

In return Billy becomes fanatically devoted to the old man, as any loveless creature would respond to kindness. When Tunstall, who believes that the only way to avoid gun trouble is to go without one, is murdered by a crooked deputy and three gunmen whom Billy sees riding away from the scene, Billy vows to avenge his friend's death. It is that thirst for vengeance that brings Billy to be killed by his friend Marshall Pat Garrett, because he believes himself when he says, "I don't run. I don't hide. I go where I want. … I do what I want."

What saves the movie even when it goes over the top is Newman's ability to shift his face and manner in a moment from guile to murderous intent to a smile of dazzling innocence. Whether the killer driven by a crazy logic or the lost boy, the smart animal under the moody surface comes through. The tragedy is fulfilled because at one level, innocence, or at least a strange kind of purity, is killed. Newman has kind words for the picture, which he felt was "a little bit ahead of its time and a classic in Europe. To this day I still get $8,000–$14,000 at the end of the year. Go to Paris right now, and I bet you it is playing in some tiny theater." (Vidal calls it "a film that only someone French could like.")

The movie version of *Cat on a Hot Tin Roof* had little to do with either innocence or purity. It also had little to do with the stage play, at least in so far as telling the audience why Brick Pollitt (Newman) is so ambivalent in his response to his wife Maggie's (Elizabeth Taylor) affections and so disdainful of his father, whose guiding wish seems to be to leave to Brick his estate of "close on 10 million in cash an' blue-chip stocks, outside, mind you, twenty-eight thousand acres of the richest land this side of the Valley Nile," over which not only Maggie but also Brick's brother, Gooper, and his wife, Mae, are salivating. When Big Daddy (Burl Ives) roars out, "Something's missing here!" amid the din and flashing of the thunder and lightning outside the house that too obviously mirror the dark and stormy night inside, he's speaking for the audience as well, because what's missing is the homosexual overtone in the relationship between Brick and his adored and recently dead friend Skipper, which in the play leads so clearly to Brick's drinking and rage. Even so, it's hard to imagine a family more generally greedy, suspicious, and hate-filled than the one that appears on the screen, or one more keenly able to insult and belittle each other at every turn.

Brick is actually and metaphorically crippled, having broken his leg while drunkenly running the hurdles at his old high school track at 2 A.M. in an effort to recapture the glory of

his youth. Maggie is known as the Cat, and the hot tin roof is the bed that she and Brick share, or, in this case, don't. Their failure to produce the children Big Daddy so desperately wants is fodder for cruel comments by others in the family. Director Richard Brooks adapted the play with James Poe, and the movie exudes Williams's rich, poisonous dialogue.

Newman's portrayal of a man who has lost both his relationship with his wife and that with his father, and can't figure out how to mend them until the closing scenes, brought him his first Academy Award nomination (Ives won the Oscar for Best Supporting Actor, but it was for his performance in *The Big Country*). The theme of a father trying to forge a relationship with his thirty-year-old son after a lifetime of what the son sees as neglect, and the son desperately wanting that bond, but suspicious and resentful of any attempt to forge it for fear of being disappointed and hurt yet again, is one Newman has played convincingly in several films. It underestimates Newman's talent to suggest that his limited relationship with his own father, or in later films the death of his son, allowed him to plumb the role however it was written, because Newman is too good an actor to rely only on direct experience. But the problems that arose from the conflictual or nonexistent father and son relations

Brick Pollitt, the way he was, the way he is, in *Cat on a Hot Tin Roof* with Big Daddy (Burl Ives) in the basement where they finally come to peace with each other. Newman received his first Academy Award nomination as Best Actor. (David Niven won for *Separate Tables*.)

experienced by Brick Pollitt and Edward W. Hall Jr. and Rocky Graziano and Billy the Kid and Hud Bannon were movingly captured by a young man who was familiar with them.

Newman has never commented directly on the causes of the unhappiness in his early life that brought on the rift with his father and brought out the anger that made him so willing to fight. Anyway, the causes are not so important as the result, and that was his marginalization, the feeling that he was somehow on the side rather than at the heart. One way or another, it seems that Newman didn't really fit in—not with his family, not at school. By his estimation, his first success was as an actor, which is to say, as being outwardly someone else who draws life from the player's inner experience. One of Newman's enduring strengths is that he can take us inside the character of an outsider. Robert Benton, who directed Newman in *Nobody's Fool*, does not pretend to know how it came about, but Newman, he says, "has a real sympathy for people who are neglected."

Cat on a Hot Tin Roof was MGM's biggest money-maker of the year and the reviews, while not unreserved raves for the picture, were so for the actors. "Paul Newman is one of the finest actors in [movies], playing cynical underacting against highly developed action," the critic for *Variety* wrote. "His command of the articulate, sensitive sequences is unmistakable, and the way he mirrors his feelings is basic to every scene."

"Mr. Newman is perhaps the most resourceful and dramatically restrained of the lot," another critic wrote. "He gives an ingratiating picture of a tortured and tested young man. Miss Taylor … is terrific as a panting, impatient wife, wanting the love of her husband as sincerely as she wants an inheritance."

Newman's Method approach to acting was well known when he made the movie. The technique stresses the importance of emotional memory and past experiences as a means to make a character's entrance not a beginning of the action but rather a continuation. The notion is that empathic observation develops a wide emotional range, and onstage actions and reactions should appear real rather than staged. This reliance on inner impulses opens the possibility for a scene to take on unexpected new directions; a turn some directors view as a threat to their control of a production. George Abbott, who recently died at the age of 107 and was a central figure in the American theater for virtually all of this century, is reported to have responded to an actor's question, "What's my motivation?" with, "Your job."

RIGHT
To spoof the perception that many in the crew had of Method acting, during rehearsals of *Cat on a Hot Tin Roof* "I suddenly tore off my pajama top and started to climb into my wife's (Elizabeth Taylor's) nightgown, crying 'Skipper! Skipper!' There were twenty people on that set and, do you know, not one of them laughed. To them, this was the Method in action, and they stood there in respectful silence."

While Newman finds the approach he learned at the Actors Studio helpful for getting inside a character, he feels that people who don't understand the process take it far too seriously. Over the course of his career he has developed a reputation as a practical joker of some substance—he had the director George Roy Hill's desk chain-sawed in two for reneging on a liquor bill; arranged for Robert Altman's deerskin gloves to be dipped in batter and deep-fried, then served to him for lunch on the set of *Buffalo Bill and the Indians*; and had a wrecked Porsche that Robert Redford had sent *him* as a joke compacted and placed in the vestibule of Redford's house—but his pleasure in a put-on was not then as widely known as was his approach to acting, which served him perfectly during the making of the movie.

"Remember Skipper, the dead friend who was supposed to be a homosexual?" Newman said a few years after *Cat on a Hot Tin Roof* was released. "Well, anyway, I'm in my pajamas [in the bathroom adjoining his and Maggie's bedroom, having just turned down Maggie's advances] and I'm supposed to slam [the] door and when I do, my wife's nightgown, hanging on the door, brushes against my face. [In the movie, he presses the gown against his face and we see anguish and longing.] So, anyway, during rehearsal, when we got to that point, I suddenly tore off my pajamaa top and started to climb into my wife's nightgown, crying, 'Skipper! Skipper!' There were twenty people on that set and, do you know, not one of them laughed. To them, this was the Method in action and they stood in respectful silence. So-o-o, having bombed out on *that* mission, I mumbled something about, well, no, I guessed I wouldn't do it that way, after all."

Paul Newman and Joanne Woodward married in Las Vegas on 29 January 1958, then honeymooned in London. She is a collector of sherry glasses and he writes poetry. For a present he gave her a sherry-sized silver cup inscribed: "So you wound up with Apollo/ If he's sometimes hard to swallow/Use this."

For some months previously, they had been living in a rented house on the beach in Malibu, with their good friend Gore Vidal. He calls them Miss Georgia and Mr. Shaker Heights, which also quite perfectly describes their stringent characterizations of *Mr. and Mrs. Bridge* (1990), in whom everything happens under the surface. India Bridge is prim, perfectly mannered and totally deferential to her husband, Walter, a lawyer who has spent his life in work. He has an opinion about everything and expects his wife, who ventures none of her own, to accept them. When a tornado alert forces everyone at their country club to take cover, Walter calmly stays at the dinner table and butters his biscuits while she looks on in fear, but stays. After the alert ends he says matter-of-factly, "For twenty years I've been telling you when something will or will not happen." On the occasion when Walter *does* worry about his mortality, he takes India to the bank to see the securities he has put away for her and their children. What might be an almost comic scene is poignant and tender.

Robert Benton says, "Walter Bridge is the most un-Paul Newman character, although he says it is the most like him of anybody. I'm not certain that's true. But he's brilliant in that movie; he has one hand tied behind his back because he's not allowed to do anything."

Newman and Woodward have appeared together in eleven pictures. He has also directed her in four others, plus the moving television version of Michael Cristopher's Pulitzer Prize-winning play *The Shadow Box* (about three patients in a Californian hospice who share their thoughts on mortality), which his daughter Susan co-produced. In each instance their films are about characters rather than star vehicles for themselves. They create an intimacy appropriate to the roles rather than one that relies on the closeness of their marriage, and they manage to exude a comfortable familarity that makes the viewer believe that these characters—as opposed to these actors—have been together for decades. Their deep knowledge of each other, Newman says, both adds to their pleasure and keeps them honest. "When we work together we both know we can't get away with any old tricks, because the other one is sitting there nodding his head knowingly and saying, 'Yes, I seem to remember doing this on the twenty-eighth page of *The Helen Morgan Story*.'" Despite the seamlessness of their performances, their approach to their art when they married could not have been more different. She was and is instinctive. He was methodical, particularly then, although forty years of experience have made him somewhat less so now; he looks back on his early work with a sense that he would sometimes "over-think" or over-prepare for a role. A mutual friend said of them a few years after their marriage, "With Joanne, you just give her the words and tell her where to stand. Paul, on the other hand, is careful, painstaking, studious, concerned with motivations."

Paul Newman and Joanne
Woodward were married
in 1958. Their friend Gore
Vidal, with whom they
shared a beach house
before their wedding,
affectionately calls them
Miss Georgia and Mr.
Shaker Heights.

"I think he's crazy," Woodward said early on in their marriage. "When he's working he breaks the whole script down … he's totally dedicated … he's awful. Won't talk. If it's a terribly difficult part, I don't see him at all. Oh, he's there, all right, but he isn't. He's off inside his head somewhere."

Soon after their marriage Newman said of Woodward, "Without her I'd be nowhere, nothing—she really opened me up." Asked about that nearly thirty-five years later he added, "I just think it was a kind of fortuitous coming together, because she had an ameliorating effect on my excesses, which were excessive enough but at least there was a partial lid put on them. And the things that set her on fire were the kinds of fires I could quell somehow. Mine were drinking, behaving badly, living too close to the edge. Why did I do that? I think it probably took a lot of pressure off in general. A safety valve."

For all the personal happiness, 1958 was a year of professional discontent. The roles he was getting were fine for the most part, but the money he was being paid was not. His Warner contract had been renewed on schedule in August 1957, raising him to $1,750 a week with a minimum guarantee of two movies and an option for a third, which meant that for *The Long, Hot Summer* and *Cat on a Hot Tin Roof* he earned $17,500 for each ten-week shoot. Nice enough pay by many standards, but not, he felt, when Warner Bros. collected $75,000 in loan-out fees for him on each movie. He made his unhappiness public in a funny but bitingly sarcastic speech at a Hollywood press luncheon while he was on loan-out to Fox for *Cat on a Hot Tin Roof*, detailing his misuse by Warner Bros. and annoying Jack Warner in the process. But there is this to be said about Newman: he was an equal opportunity annoyer. He irked the gossip columnists as well by refusing to talk about his private life, which the studios expected their stars to do (so long as they told the right parts). Newman's opinion was and is that if he did his job right, then he exposed himself enough on camera. What he wore to bed and what he did in his spare time was his own business.

He kept a low profile even at work. One day in 1971, during the filming of *The Towering Inferno* on the Twentieth Century-Fox lot, the writer David Freeman was walking back to work after lunch in what was generally acknowledged as the nicest studio commissary in town. "Parked by a soundstage was a beautiful silver Porsche with PN license plates," he recalls. "And behind the wheel was Newman, eating a commissary lunch. It didn't look like fun at all to be so recognizable. And that was on a movie lot!"

Away from the studio, Newman sometimes wore a false beard and sunglasses to disguise himself when he went for a walk, which worked with varying success. Disguised or not, there is, he feels, a basic right that "you should be allowed to speak with your wife without interruption if you care to; I care to. I care to walk down Fifth Avenue without—sometimes on request, sometimes on demand—putting my name on a piece of paper or standing for a photograph with someone's favorite dog or family baby. When people say, 'Smile,' or 'Take off your dark glasses,' I immediately think of a drill instructor ordering me around."

Even so, for many years he would graciously inscribe his name for an admirer, despite feeling intruded upon. But he stopped after an absurd situation put the act in perspective.

"I gave up signing autographs," he explained to Peter S. Greenberg in a *Playboy* interview some years ago, "when I was standing at a urinal at Sardi's and a guy came up to me with a piece of paper and a pen in his hand. Since that moment, I've thought about the foolishness of it and the indecency of it and realized there was no situation that could not be violated. . . . I wondered . . . what do I do with my hands? Do I wash them first and shake hands? Or do I shake hands and then wash up?"

It is the same when people ask him to take off his sunglasses so they can see if his eyes are really *that* blue; it is one of those things that fans seem to think stars owe them. Newman agrees that he owes his audience something, but not that. "I owe them a lot. I owe them the best performance I can give; I owe them an appearance on my set exactly on time; I owe them trying to work for the best I can, not just for money. But if somebody says what I owe him is to stand up against a wall and take off my dark glasses so he can take a picture of my baby blues, then I say, 'No, I don't owe you that.' I try not to be hurtful. I say something like, 'If I take off my glasses, my pants will fall down.' Or, if they're insistent, I say, 'Sure, I'll take off my dark glasses if you'll let me look at your gums.' Fair's fair. . . . The blue eye stuff is offensive because of the implication that you'd be a failure if you didn't have them: 'That's how you made it so take off your glasses so we can see your famous blue eyes.' It's like with Bo Derek, you know: 'Take off your brassière so we can check your boobs.' It has exactly the same connotation; there's something of a put-down to it."

Knowing that people perceive him according to his appearance on the screen, Newman says, has made him "suspicious. I suppose that's why most of my friends are people I've known for twenty or twenty-five years. John Foreman, the producer, once gave a description of me that I love and cherish. He said, 'Paul Newman gets up every morning, walks to the window, and scans the horizon for enemies.'"

He is even more vehement about the privacy of his marriages. His response has always been, "It's simply nobody's business." "What happened to us during that period is not going to help anybody live a happy life—it's not going to help people's marriages, it's not going to destroy their marriages—and it's simply nobody's business," he said in 1983. "This is the great age of candor, the age of ... the *National Enquirer*, but my theme for the Eighties is 'Fuck candor.' It even inspired me to write a poem—just one. I call it *The Age of Candor*:

Is mystery there?

Penthouse—

Hustler

Spread—

Wide.

World Wide

Viva, Screw!

Do these invest a head

with magic speculation?

Well ...

I talk more to lust

with veils and shadows

In darkness

layers peeled

Each tactile step

Read not in kilowatts

The intimation of ...

suggests

my private wonder."

We are left to our private wonder as to most of the details of the Newman-Woodward marriage, which are their business, anyway. There are, however, a few details that they have talked about: like every other couple, they have arguments but aren't defeated by them. At one point in their marriage Newman packed a bag and moved out, only to return ten minutes later because he realized that he had no place to go to. They laugh a lot. She calls him the best director she has worked for, which could even be true. He likes to direct her in films because, as their friend, the writer Stewart Stern, says, "Paul has a sense of real adoration for what Joanne can do. He's constantly trying to provide a setting where the world can see what he sees in her."

He calls her "the last of the big-time broads," which is a compliment. He says they are equals but that sometimes he forgets "how incredible she is." That is remedied by so simple a thing as looking around their Manhattan apartment, which is decorated with elegant antiques and chintz-covered couches. In 1986 he said with some amazement, "If anyone had ever told me twenty years ago I'd be sitting in a room with peach walls, I would have told them to take a nap in a urinal." When in 1969 the widely read gossip columnist Joyce Haber reported without checking its accuracy that the Newmans "are already living apart, according to friends, and will get a divorce," the couple took out a $3,000 half-page ad in the *Los Angeles Times*:

(1) Recognizing the power of the press—

(2) Fearing to embarrass an awesome journalist—

(3) Terrified to disappoint Miss Haber and her readers, we will try to accommodate her "Fascinating Rumors, So Far Unchecked" by busting up our marriage even though we still like each other.

Joanne and Paul Newman

OVERLEAF
Mr. Shaker Heights and Miss Georgia and friend at home on the range not long after their marriage. His enjoyment of cooking led to the Newman's Own line of foods, and so far nearly $70 million in charitable donations.

NEWMAN

The Early Years

RIGHT
Newman c. 1958.

LEFT
Newman c. 1959,
around the time he
made *The Young
Philadelphians.*

Lobby card for *The Long, Hot Summer* (1958), the first of eleven films that Newman and Joanne Woodward have so far acted in together.

As Ben Quick with Will Varner (Orson Welles) in *The Long, Hot Summer*.

As Brick Pollitt with his wife Maggie the Cat (Elizabeth Taylor) in the somewhat declawed film version of *Cat on a Hot Tin Roof* (1958).

ABOVE
**Paul Newman and Joanne Woodward
around the time of their marriage in 1958.**

RIGHT
**Newman and Joanne
Woodward—in
contrast to her
character, who for
most of *From the
Terrace* (1960) is
brittle and cold.**

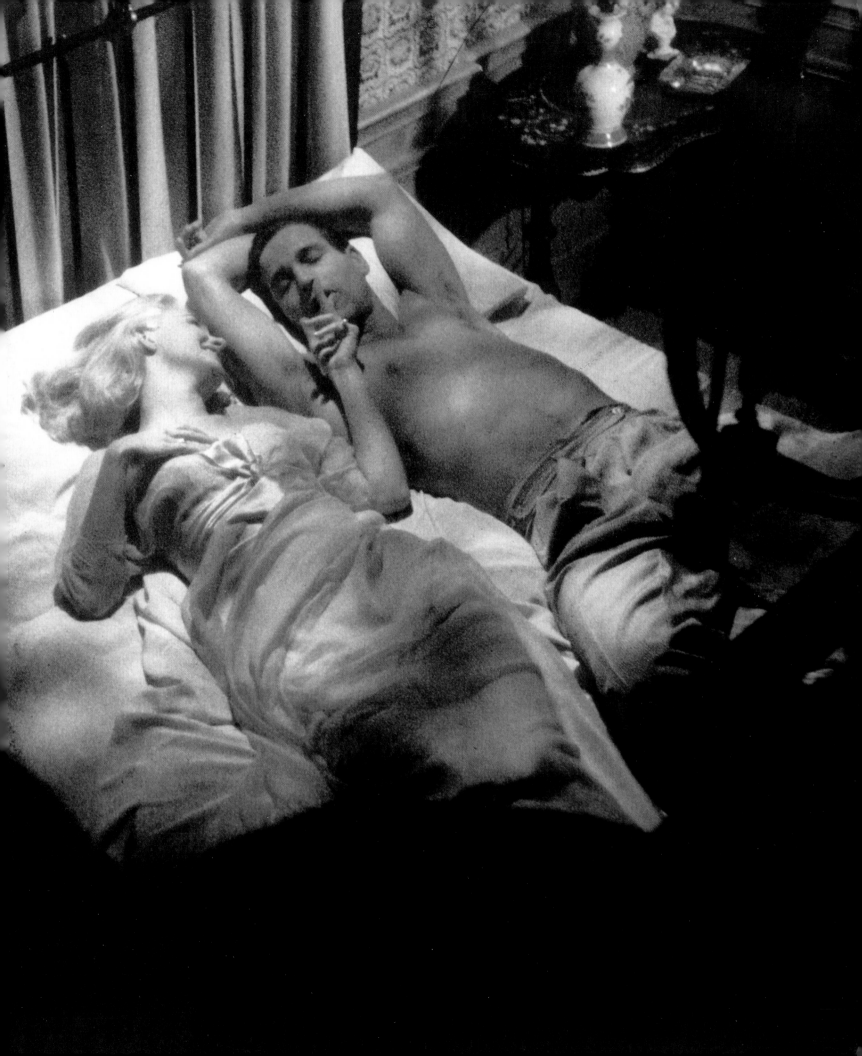

ABOVE
At home with Joanne Woodward in 1965.

ABOVE RIGHT
On the set of *Exodus* (1960), in which he played Ari Ben Canaan. What the film demonstrates, in comparison with other Newman pictures, is how much his real power is displayed in portrayals of more complex and less overtly heroic men.

BELOW RIGHT
Newman's famed whimsical acts seem to come off the top of his head. Other whimsical things alight on it.

PAUL NEWMAN IS "HUD"!

THE MAN WITH THE BARBED WIRE SOUL!

"Superbly acted...magnificently filmed..."
—BOB CONSIDINE

A SALEM-DOVER PRODUCTION

co-starring MELVYN DOUGLAS · PATRICIA NEAL · BRANDON deWILDE

PANAVISION® · PRODUCED BY MARTIN RITT and IRVING RAVETCH · DIRECTED BY MARTIN RITT

SCREENPLAY BY IRVING RAVETCH and HARRIET FRANK, JR. · FROM A NOVEL BY LARRY McMURTRY · MUSIC SCORED BY ELMER BERNSTEIN

A PARAMOUNT RELEASE

63/117

ABOVE
In *Lady L* (1965), with Sophia
Loren, in which he played a
comical anarchist. "I woke up
every morning and knew I wasn't
cutting the mustard."

LEFT
Lobby card for *Hud* (1963). Actually,
Paul Newman isn't at all like the
self-absorbed Hud Bannon.

They lived in a series of rented houses and apartments—Newman estimates there were ten in the first four years of their marriage—when not on location for films. In 1958 the two of them made another picture together, this one, *Rally Round the Flag, Boys!*, a send-up of suburban life adapted from Max Shulman's novel. A sharp, satiric farceur, Shulman is one of the greatest American humorists; countless writers have tried to emulate his graceful, hilarious, seemingly meringue-like prose, with dismal and leaden results. But books are one thing, movies another. The story concerns a Connecticut housewife (Woodward) who spends the day on community affairs rather than good housekeeping. After their town is selected as a missile site, she sends her husband (Newman) to fight the decision in Washington, D. C., where he is followed with predictable misunderstanding by their sexy neighbor (Joan Collins).

Leo McCarey, the director, had impeccable credentials for the job: he wrote and directed many of Laurel and Hardy's best silents, he directed W. C. Fields, the Marx Brothers in *Duck Soup*, and *An Affair to Remember*. Still, *Rally Round the Flag, Boys!* was flat and unfunny, and Newman's opinion is that his performance was "weak."

Putting aside how much more, say, Cary Grant was suited for the role, part of Newman's trouble may have been his increasing dissatisfaction with how Warner Bros. was treating him. Once again he was lent out at great profit to the studio but not to him. The Warner

Woodward and Newman on the set of *Rally Round the Flag, Boys!* (1958), enjoying all the glamour of filmmaking.

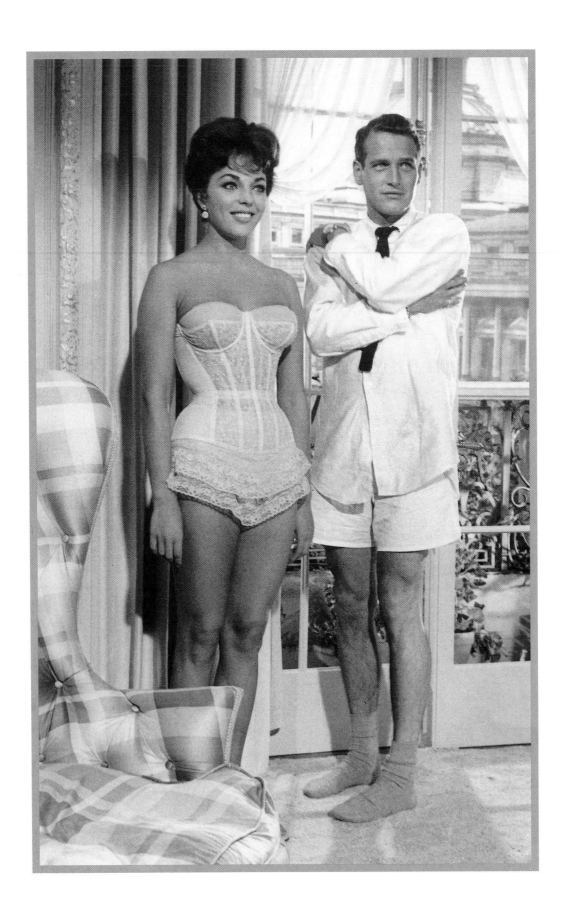

agreement with Fox paid Newman $1,750 a week while Warner Bros. pocketed $7,500 a week for a minimum of ten weeks, with the eleventh week free. Fox had to carry Workman's Compensation on him and give him "a so-called 'star dressing room' as such term is understood in the motion picture industry." He was also to have star or costar billing, and first position of the entire cast in print ads, with his name in the size of type of the title. This is one way in which Hollywood keeps score, and Newman was doing fine on that side of the ledger. The other side is what a star earns, and here he wasn't. When in August, Warner Bros. made their annual renewal of his contract, raising his salary $250 a week, to $2,000, all it did was drive home how much money he was making for the studio, and by comparison how little he was making for himself.

He would no doubt have been happy to know when he reported for work on *The Young Philadelphians* in late 1958 that it was the last movie he would have to make for Warner Bros., or for anybody else. The result was perfectly respectable and a great example of the kind of movies made in the late 1950s. But what it best serves to do is demonstrate why the studio mentality worked against Newman coming into himself. He was cast as a decent young man of social prominence but no money who earns his tuition for law school by working in construction, thereby requiring him to have his shirt off for several scenes. The script covers every base: smart, attractive young man with difficult past gets and then loses girl, becomes tough and cynical, then finds redemption—and the girl—by risking everything for a friend. The problem is that there is no grain in the character for Newman to work against.

Newman's narration over the opening of the movie was prophetic: "A man's life, they say, is the sum of his actions." His own actions over the next few months would give considerable shape to his life. When, shortly after making *The Young Philadelphians*, Warner Bros. reneged on an agreement for Newman to do a picture for another studio, the actor met with Jack Warner and demanded that Warner Bros. allow him to buy back his contract. It was an act of either great bravery or unremitting foolishness.

"I told Jack Warner to go fuck himself—and this was very early in the game when I really couldn't afford to tell him to go fuck himself," Newman says. "But I really didn't give a damn."

LEFT
In a less compromising position than meets the eye in *Rally Round the Flag, Boys!* (1958). After their small town is selected as a missile site, Newman is sent to Washington by his wife (Woodward) to fight the decision. When their sexy neighbor (Joan Collins) follows him there, the predictable misunderstanding ensues.

A few established stars, Kirk Douglas and Bette Davis among them, had fought the studios by refusing to appear in movies they had no desire to do, and were willing to take a financial loss to get control of their work. Their defiance had impressed Newman. When Warner stalled in his response to Newman's demand, Newman played his only trump card and exercised his option to do a Broadway play, which opened on 10 March 1959.

It was the perfect move. The play was Tennessee Williams's *Sweet Bird of Youth*, the other lead was Geraldine Page, the director was Elia Kazan, and the success was unmitigated.

Chance Wayne (Newman), a gigolo with acting ambitions who is currently attached to The Princess Kosmonopolis (Page), an ageing movie queen, returns to his home town where, years before and unbeknownst to him, he had left his girlfriend pregnant and infected with syphilis. She was forced to have both an abortion and a hysterectomy. When her despotic political-boss father, Thomas J. Finley, discovers that the man who ruined his daughter is back in town, he sends a vigilante party that includes his son Tom Jr. to castrate Chance. Rather than run off to Hollywood as planned with the actress, whose career has taken an upturn, if only in her vanity, Chance stays to greet his fate.

The critic Walter Kerr wrote that Newman's ambiguous character was "half vulgar greed, half yearning idealism—recklessly balanced on the slopes of hell."

Brooks Atkinson was also impressed. "The three major characters—a dissipated movie star, a blackmailing gigolo, a political boss—are malignant and malevolent, giving and receiving pain, doomed to destruction. The characters of Dostoevski and Faulkner are the nearest equivalents to Mr. Williams's own gallery of persons. ... Paul Newman's characterization of the reckless young man is excellent. ... Beneath the young man's cheap pretensions, the characterization retains a trace of decency from the past." He called the play "brilliantly acted," adding, "Miss Page is at the peak of form in this characterization. And Paul Newman's young man is the perfect companion-piece. Although he has a braggart, calculating exterior, he is as immature as an adolescent; brassy outside, terrified and remorseful when he stops strutting."

In an essay on Williams that appeared shortly after the play opened, Atkinson continued, "When Mr. Williams first came into the theater, he had a feeling of tenderness toward his characters. *The Glass Menagerie* is a tender play; it is filled with compassion for the maimed, the sick and the doomed. *A Streetcar Named Desire* communicated feelings of sympathy for

Blanche Du Bois's shattering misfortune … But Mr. Williams plunged into later plays violently. *Cat on a Hot Tin Roof*, *Orpheus Descending* and *Garden District* are infiltrated with hate. Mr. Williams seemed to be under some sort of compulsion to punish his audiences as well as his characters. He shared the cruelty and hatred of the characters. …

"But there are moments of truth in *Sweet Bird of Youth* when the two main characters understand themselves. … Mr. Williams spares his characters nothing. But he does give them the dignity of knowledge of themselves, and he pities them as people who are lost to hells of their own choosing."

Williams's creations Brick Pollitt and Chance Wayne highlighted Newman's ability to elicit a sense of compassion from the audience for men who at first and even second glance are unworthy of it. Williams was such a powerful force in the theater of the time, and Newman's talent for bringing his characters to multilayered life was so good, that one would assume there was a more than passing relationship between writer and actor. But even though each did so much for the other artistically, including Newman directing Joanne

Newman had hits on and off Broadway while performing in *Sweet Bird of Youth* in 1959.

Woodward in a movie of *The Glass Menagerie* (1987), they did not know each other very well offstage. Still, Newman was present when a critical change was made in *Sweet Bird of Youth*, which also serves to show how much a play can alter in tryouts.

"I never got to know Tennessee Williams more than as a guy who came to rehearsals and did not seem at all like a poet to me," Newman said in 1994. "Of course the big problem in *Sweet Bird* is, when does Chance get the information [that the thugs are on the way to get him]? Everyone knew it was supposed to be at the end of the second act but nobody knew how to do it or how it would happen. We got to Philadelphia, and I think at 7:42 they handed me twelve pages and said, 'This is going on tonight, walk around with it.'

"And I said, 'You can't give him the information at the end of the first act. You can't play the rest of the play. You can't play the second act if he knows this.'

"So I went on and of course it didn't work. And [afterwards] there was a party, I think at somebody's house by the name of Gimble, and Josh Logan was there. It's my memory again—my pilot and radioman, we traded off the turret on a torpedo bomber, and the three of us got together and we couldn't agree on one thing on World War II, so I'm not sure that *Sweet Bird of Youth* is going to be any more accurate—but my memory is that we were all sort of standing around in a circle discussing why that first act ending didn't work and how we were going to get the information to Chance. And Kazan was standing there and Tennessee and myself and Josh Logan, and Josh said, 'Why doesn't Tom tell him?'

"And someone said, 'That's crazy, he's going to cut his nuts off at the end of the play.'

"And Tennessee said, 'Good-bye!'" Newman said with a big laugh, "and just hightailed out of the room. The next morning we had the second act."

The play ran for forty-two weeks, during which time two major events in the Newman family took place. In April 1959, shortly after *Sweet Bird of Youth* opened, Joanne Woodward delivered the first of the three daughters of their marriage, Elinor Theresa, nicknamed Nell Potts. Then, that August, Newman's Luck returned its attention to his career.

Newman's agent at the time was Lew Wasserman, until recently the Chief Executive Officer of MCA, the parent company of Universal Studios, and for decades one of the most powerful men in the movie business. Even in 1959 Wasserman had great clout. He also had a great sense of what his client's worth was. When Newman came to him and complained of his frustration in being a contract player and expressed his desire to get out of his Warner Bros. contract, Wasserman had a plan. He suggested to Newman that he offer Jack Warner $500,000 to buy out his remaining years of servitude. Newman thought Wasserman was crazy, that it would take him twenty years to pay it off.

"Let me handle it," Wasserman told him.

Wasserman waited for the appropriate moment. He felt that it had arrived when one day Warner was in a foul temper in anticipation that Newman would be difficult regarding his next assignment. Like Aesop's fox tricking the crow into dropping the meat, Wasserman is reported to have said, "Why don't you let Newman buy up his contract? He'll never amount to much."

Warner took the bait—and the money. In August 1959 all parties signed an agreement terminating Newman's obligations to Warner Bros. in exchange for $500,000, to be paid "without interest by giving an amount equal to the total gross compensation and royalties, without deductions, paid to the artist with respect to any and all engagements of the artist," with the exception through 5 January 1960 (the day he was to leave the show) of his salary for the Broadway production of *Sweet Bird of Youth*.

Although he had no way to know it at the time, Newman would pay off the debt in less than two years. What he did know was that he was free of Warner Bros., among the most active of the studios in terms of number of movies made, but probably the least concerned about the overall careers of its stars. Many contract players who began with promise soon disappeared into the dark hole of bad roles and became trivia questions. Newman had fared reasonably well so far at Warner Bros., but now his career was in his own more caring hands, and the buyout was both professionally and personally liberating.

During the end of the run of *Sweet Bird of Youth* he and Woodward began filming *From the Terrace* by day while he continued to perform at the Martin Beck Theater at night. It was their third movie together, this one from the sprawling John O'Hara novel that explores human frailties and foibles in love, marriage and business. The movie concerns Alfred Eaton (Newman), the son of an emotionally destroyed alcoholic mother (Myrna Loy) and a millionaire father (Leon Ames) whose compassion died with his first son and now is inversely proportionate to his wealth. Alfred's relationship with his parents is nicely set up at the beginning of the movie, when he returns home from World War II to find his mother drunk and his father as warm as winter.

"My boy. Home at last," his father says with no emotion.

"Hello, Father."

"'Hello, Father.' Is that all after all this time?"

"No. There's a lot more."

"Yes, I should think there would be. … "

"How was the war?"

"OK, I guess. We won."

As his mother totters upstairs to bed, she says, "Goodnight, Alfred. Sleep as late as you like. And remember, you're coming home tomorrow. Tonight never happened."

A maid comes into the living room, where he is standing alone while his father berates his mother upstairs.

"Well, Mr. Alfred," she asks. "How does it feel to be home again and seeing your mother and father?"

"Things don't change, Nellie. They just get more so."

But the meat of the movie is the relationship between Alfred and his wife, the former Mary St. John (Woodward), whose own prosperous family looks upon the Eatons as *nouveau riche* nobodies. At the beginning of the movie Mary is engaged to a very suitable psychiatrist, at least until the following scene when she and Alfred are alone and wrapped up in each other:

"Alfred, are you going to do something? And be somebody?"

"For you?"

"Yes."

"Settle down?"

"Yes."

"With you?" he asks. Her response is to kiss him wildly.

"Love me?" he asks again.

"Oh, I want you more than anything in the world. [She is still kissing him.] You're never going to want anybody else as long as you live."

RIGHT
Newman played Alfred Eaton by day as he filmed *From the Terrace* with Joanne Woodward, and Chance Wayne by night on Broadway in *Sweet Bird of Youth*. During breaks on the set, he and Woodward could just be themselves.

If that were true, the movie would have ended in the third reel. Instead, audiences were treated to an examination by two actors in fine form of the price of success and its ugly marital effects. Should Alfred, who puts in the marriage-killing travel necessary to build a socially prominent business career, stay married to his restless wife, who returns to her old beau for comfort while Alfred is away, and quite likes the arrangement? Or should he give up the rat race and settle down with a sweet small-town girl (Ina Balin), whom he meets on a trip and who loves him for himself? Woodward is quite wonderful as the sensual and self-ish wife. For his part, Newman plays the combination of hurt son driven to best his father in business, and cheated husband, with a sense of decency and strength of character that makes satisfying an ending whose lesson is to be true to oneself.

Woodward as the sensuous, selfish Mary St. John, and Newman as Alfred Eaton, who sees his marriage disintegrating as the cost of his success.

When *Exodus* was released in December 1960, five months after *From the Terrace*, audiences saw Newman in his first completely heroic role. He played Ari Ben Canaan, the isolationist leader of the Palestinian underground, who masterminds the escape by sea of 600 Jews from British-blockaded Cyprus to the promised land of Palestine. The three-and-a-half-hour spectacle, in Super-Panavision and Technicolor, about the birth of the State of Israel in 1947–48 was adapted from Leon Uris's novel by Dalton Trumbo. Otto Preminger directed the big-star cast, that included Eva Marie Saint, Ralph Richardson, Lee J. Cobb, Peter Lawford, Sal Mineo and Hugh Griffith. Newman as an unambiguous champion is fine in a conventional way, but any number of handsome actors could have played Ari. What *Exodus* demonstrates by comparison with other Newman movies is how much his real power is displayed in portrayals of more complex and less overtly heroic men.

The film was shot in Israel, so the entire Newman family packed up and went en masse, as is generally their custom. Newman and Woodward have had to endure few long separations, "due as much to Joanne's intelligence as my insistence," he says. "She's had many opportunities to go abroad or on location by herself, and she's turned these offers down in order to stay with me; she's done this to the detriment of her career, I'm afraid, but it's helped us keep together."

Despite the comfort of being with Woodward, and even though his fee was now $200,000 a picture, making *Exodus* was by all accounts an unpleasant job. "Chilly," is Newman's summation. One obvious explanation is that there are few stars and directors more unsuited to each other than were Newman and Preminger. Newman is always interested in discussing details of his character. Preminger was interested only in actors doing simply what he told them to do. When Newman reportedly took several pages of suggestions regarding Ari to Preminger, Preminger airily said they were "very interesting" and then dismissed Newman with, "If you were directing the picture, you would use them. As I am directing the picture, I shan't use them."

Perhaps that is why one reviewer wrote, "Ari Ben Canaan, the foremost hero, who is forcefully, albeit it much too neatly, played by an always well-shaved Paul Newman, is a mighty stout fellow to have around, quick and sure with the command decisions, but it is hard to gather precisely where he stands or what distinguishes him as an individual from

In a classic confusion of character with actor, some people who saw Newman shoot pool after he made *The Hustler* were surprised that he couldn't play as well as Fast Eddie Felson.

any other fellow who would naturally be attracted to Eva Marie Saint." Still, audiences jammed the theaters to see *Exodus*. It turned out to be the biggest-grossing Newman movie to that time.

However unhappy the making of *Exodus*, this was a very successful period for him. Newman had gained his independence, his fees had soared, and so too had his popularity. While *Exodus* was an inauspicious start artistically to a new decade, the '60s would provide him with many of his most memorable roles. Besides Newman's four H films—*The Hustler* (1961), *Hud* (1963), *Harper* (1966), and *Hombre* (1967)—there were also *Cool Hand Luke* (1967), *Butch Cassidy and the Sundance Kid* (1969), and his debut as a feature movie director in *Rachel, Rachel* (1968).

The Hustler is one of those movies that become so much a part of popular culture that it is remembered and referred to even by people who have never seen it. It also marks the first of the roles that are completely Paul Newman's. Newman *is* Fast Eddie, and no one else could ever be. His total association with him is what made *The Color of Money* so moving and successful; it was not a sequel but rather a pickup of a life twenty-five years later. What is perhaps most remarkable is that Eddie Felson is just one of at least four roles Newman played in the 1960s that are equally synonymous with him—Harper, Cool Hand Luke, and Butch Cassidy being the others.

A great strength of the movie is the dialogue, written by director Robert Rossen and Sidney Carroll. Jackie Gleason as Minnesota Fats, Piper Laurie as the crippled Sarah Packard, and George C. Scott who, as one critic put it, played the gambler Bert Gordon "as though the devil himself had donned dark glasses and taken up residence in a rancid billiard hall," take the audience through the darkest side of life in a compelling story of greed, evil, and brutal reality, with a little redemption at the end.

What particularly interested Newman in both Eddie and Chance Wayne was what he calls the "corruptibility level" of a man, or of a nation. Here were men in whom the seed of corruption had flourished, and how and why that happened fascinated him. Newman's strength is to bring light to the kaleidoscope of tensions and forces in people like Reggie Dunlop, the ageing hockey player-coach in *Slap Shot*; or Frank Galvin, the alcoholic lawyer in *The Verdict*; or the stuffy and bigoted Walter Bridge. Unlike Brando or Dean, who created bravura performances of epochal characters like Terry Malloy, the ex-prizefighter in *On the Waterfront*, and Jim, the juvenile delinquent in *Rebel Without a Cause*, Newman is best in movies where he plays more common men who have unexpected depth.

Even though he was pleased at the time, Newman has for many years been dissatisfied with his performance as Fast Eddie. He saw some segments about twenty years after making the movie and was "very conscious of working too hard, which comes partly from lack of faith in your own talent and lack of faith that just doing it in itself is all that the audience requires."

George C. Scott long ago agreed with Newman's self-assessment, and said in interviews after the movie was released that he wasn't impressed with Newman's acting. Publicly, anyway, Newman was unfazed.

"I don't think I'd have been very impressed, either," he said in 1983. "I was just working too hard, showing too much," a criticism he would never make of Scott. "He's electric. Unpredictable, with a marvelous sense of threat and danger, which was so great for his part in *The Hustler*. He was on Broadway recently, playing a light Noël Coward role, and it just split my skull, because he was so outrageous and delicious. He was the wrong man in the wrong part doing it absolutely *right*."

Newman received his second Academy Award nomination for Best Actor for *The Hustler*, but the Oscar went to Maximilian Schell for *Judgment at Nuremberg.* His feeling that he had worked too hard at the characterization did not really gel for some years, and at the time he was hopeful that he would win.

"I was really hurt by that one. I thought old Fast Eddie was a fairly original character," he said in 1968. The Newmans were living in Beverly Hills at the time, and Paul drove home in disappointment, which he says was soon mitigated. "Being the perfect therapist, Joanne dragged me out by the hand to the garage. We had a little hideaway out there really away from the family. She said, 'We're going to take a little caviar and a little champagne out there and watch a very bad show on television.' We never got around to the show."

He would be nominated six times before finally winning on the seventh, for *The Color of Money* in 1986. He learned the news in the same way the rest of the world did, while watching on television, at home in New York. "I've been there six times and lost," he said of his reason to stay put. "Maybe if I stay away, I'll win." The year before, he had been given an honorary award for his distinguished but Oscarless film career, and "for his personal integrity and dedication to his craft."

He nearly decided to refuse it. "He said they'd always treated him as second," Newman's friend Irving I. Axelrad told *The New York Times*, "and now they were acting as if he was old and through."

Newman's only public comment was to say that he would have preferred to have had the award for a specific piece of work. "It did ruin a great moment," he joked. "In my eighty-seventh year, having been denied an Oscar since 1952, I would have been carried up to the stage on a stretcher. Then, reaching my wizened hand out, I would have grabbed the statue and cackled, 'Thank you, finally.'"

He accepted on videotape from Chicago, where he was filming *The Color of Money*. "I am especially grateful that this did not come wrapped in a gift certificate to Forest Lawn," he said in acceptance. "I hope that my best work is down the pike, ahead of me and not behind." *The Color of Money*, *Mr. and Mrs. Bridge*, *Fat Man and Little Boy* and *Nobody's Fool*, among other movies, have assured that.

Picking those parts and fighting for the offbeat ones like Walter Bridge that are new and special and not simply "Paul Newman" roles is a challenge for Newman, as it is for any actor who creates a memorable character and then receives baskets of similar scripts. Movies cost tens of millions of dollars, and Hollywood tries to protect its investment by offering up as much of a sure thing as possible. Newman's enjoyment of the parts and the success of *Hud* and *Harper* and *Cool Hand Luke* did not diminish his awareness of the repetition in the roles.

"There are few actors who can avoid that," he said not long before *Butch Cassidy* was released. "Only the great, great actors have an inexhaustible source of variety. Brando, when he's really on, when he's interested, when he's involved, can do it. So can Olivier and

Newman taking a cue from the pool great Willie Mosconi, his coach for the technique that his character Eddie Felson required in *The Hustler*.

Guinness. My wife, Joanne, can do it. But not me, because I'm running out of steam. Wherever I look, I find parts reminiscent of Luke or Hud or Fast Eddie. Christ, I played those parts once and parts of them *more* than once. It's not only dangerous to repeat yourself, it's damned tiresome."

But actors can only play the parts that are offered to them, and then they have to see themselves in that part. Newman turned down the lead of *All That Jazz*, failing, he says, to consider how much the director Bob Fosse would bring to it. He routinely refuses parts that contain what he considers mindless violence, and so declined the very popular action comedy *Romancing the Stone*. *The Verdict* (1982) was supposed to star Robert Redford. It was only after Redford dropped out (because he didn't want the bright but hard-luck lawyer Frank Galvin to have so many unpleasant edges) that the role was offered to Newman, who immediately accepted. Galvin's dissipation is exactly what appealed to him; it allowed him to be someone quite different. "For the first time in a long time," he says, "I wasn't playing Paul Newman playing Paul Newman." Instead he gave a moving portrayal of a raspy-voiced, alcohol-ravaged man of decency who grasps at perhaps his last chance for salvation. The trouble is, Newman points out, parts like that are uncommon. "If an actor waited for beautiful scripts, he'd work once every three or four years. … I think most of the movies I've done have been pretty good but … increasingly in the past few years … I haven't found as much originality in my parts as I've been looking for. Depth and detail, yes; but not too much originality."

By biding his time in the past dozen years and waiting three or four years if necessary for an original part, Newman has been able to play more than what he calls the "flawed rakes" that people associate with him. It was three years between the return of Eddie Felson in *The Color of Money* and the appearance of lusty Earl Long in *Blaze*, who was followed immediately by the flint-eyed, gravel-voiced, win-at-all-costs General Leslie Groves in *Fat Man and Little Boy*, a man who is relentless, unsympathetic, and completely engrossing. It was two more years before Walter Bridge in *Mr. and Mrs. Bridge* and four more before he became the comically villainous business executive Sidney J. Mussberger in *The Hudsucker Proxy* (1994), but then Donald "Sully" Sullivan and *Nobody's Fool* came right after. Newman feels there is a responsibility for an actor to balance his life with his work and that he has not done this as well as some. He makes clear his high regard for actors such as George C. Scott, but he has said he is particularly envious of Laurence Olivier.

"If I envy anything, it's more the way a person lives than the way he performs. [Olivier] always seemed to be able to balance his existence between stage and screen; because there seemed to be in him enough facets—either of his own personality or his fantasy life—to be able to draw from. He didn't exhaust those facets. He dared more. Whereas I—I seem to have run out of my own skin fairly early. I seem to have exhausted my ability to create something new after a short duration as a performer. I catch myself in movies doing mannerisms that once were successful. If you find that you're just falling back on successful responses, then it's unsatisfying. Unconsciously, you feel an attitude of dismissal or boredom that encroaches on your own approach."

What Newman considers even a greater challenge than finding a wonderfully drawn character is to bring something special to even the most poorly written ones. "There are so many different things an actor looks for and finds, in terms of satisfaction," he says. "If you're under contract and you're given a terrible script and make it at least mediocre, you can say, 'This is a great achievement.' It's actually no less of an achievement than a picture like *The Hustler*, which had a marvelous script and a great character with thickness and dimension. There was so much in *that* part that I went to the studio every day muttering, 'I've got five different ways to play this thing.' Playing Harper was a ball for the same reason—a character who would absorb any kind of dramatic invention I could give him."

Alas, Ram Bowen, the trombonist he played in *Paris Blues* (1961), was not such a sop. Ram and his buddy Eddie Cook (Sidney Poitier) are a couple of footloose American jazz musicians who meet a pair of suburban American women (Joanne Woodward and Diahann Carroll) visiting France for a two-week vacation. They nearly bag the boys, but in the end, Bowen says in a particularly silly line, "Baby, I love music, morning, noon, and night. D'ya dig?" Actually, the music—Louis Armstrong is among the players—is the highlight of the picture.

In 1962, fed up with the insular nature of Hollywood and the intrusion of the public and press into their relationship and marriage, Newman, Woodward, and their two daughters, Elinor and Melissa, moved from a Beverly Hills house with a garden and pool into a

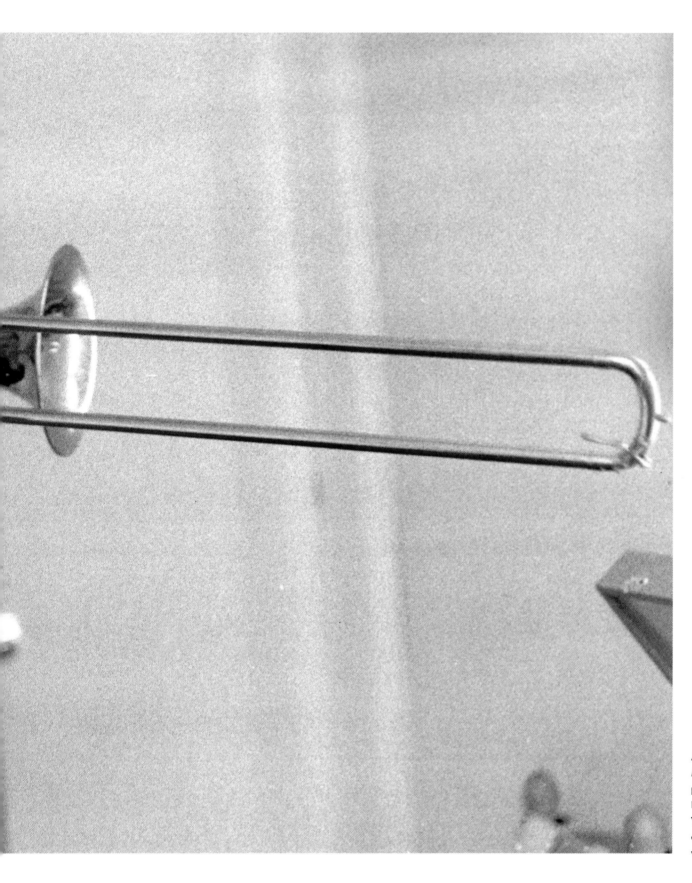

As Ram Bowen in *Paris Blues* (1961) Newman played a man who loves Lillian Corning (Joanne Woodward), but jazz even more. Off the set was another matter.

charming, low-ceilinged, 1736 farmhouse on a couple of wooded acres by the Aspetuk River in Westport, Connecticut, about ninety minutes from Manhattan. Over the years Newman has helped build a spillway, and one crosses the water via an arched suspension that resembles a tiny, green Golden Gate Bridge—he calls it "Newman's Folly."

Across the bridge is an old barn converted into a combination screening room, entertainment area and hideaway, filled with photographs and other mementoes. Over the large fireplace is a huge painting of Newman as Buffalo Bill, from his 1976 movie *Buffalo Bill and the Indians*. A house nearby, of approximately equal age to the residence, is used as a guest house. Shortly after moving to the property Newman sent out a polite enquiry through a third party to see whether the then owner of the other house might some day want to sell. If so, he hoped to purchase it so that another buyer wouldn't come along and possibly cut down some of the adjoining woods and diminish their privacy. The owner turned out to be an

Joanne Woodward won the 1957 Oscar for Best Actress for her portrayal of a young woman with multiple personalities and three separate lives in *The Three Faces of Eve*. She has had three subsequent nominations, two of them in films made with her husband —*Rachel, Rachel* (1968), which he directed, and *Mr. and Mrs. Bridge* (1990), in which he costarred.

elderly lady of proper breeding, and her response, he says, was a disdainful, "Isn't he in show business?" In time she came to appreciate the Newmans despite their line of work, and a few years ago the sale was made.

The Connecticut home would allow not only room for the three Newman-Woodward daughters, but also space for his other three children, one of whom found a name for it.

"When we bought the house and we came back from Los Angeles, I hadn't seen the older kids for a while," Newman says. "We were describing the place to them. They said, 'My gosh, it sounds marvelous.' We had been trying to think of a name for it. Suzie, who at that time must have been about nine, said, 'Well, it sounds like it's got a lot of nooks and crannies in it. Why don't you call it Nook House?' I said, 'Nook House it is.'"

Included among the furnishings was the huge brass bed Paul and Joanne had bought in New Orleans while making *The Long, Hot Summer*, an appliance Tennessee Williams once described as nineteenth-century bordello. "Three could sleep in it comfortably," Newman said after the move. "We figure it must have once stood in a cathouse; there'd be no other reason to make a bed that big." They also bought a Greenwich

Newman and his "Noscar," given him by the cast and crew of *Somebody Up There Likes Me*. He has had eight Best Actor nominations, but as far as the Academy of Motion Picture Arts and Sciences were concerned, he wasn't even a contender.

Village duplex and filled it with American antiques. On the mantel were Woodward's 1957 Best Actress Oscar for *The Three Faces of Eve* and a close facsimile of an Oscar given to Newman by everyone connected with *Somebody Up There Likes Me*, who felt he deserved to receive it for his 1956 performance as Rocky Graziano (Newman was not nominated and Yul Brynner won for *The King and I*).

The move east was prompted in part, Newman says, by trying to keep a sense of proportion in their lives. "You start making more money than you have ever thought existed. First you buy a mansion so big that even the rooms have rooms. Your children have individual governesses. ... Comes April 15 and the income-tax people want $200,000. You call your agent and the only scripts available are real dogs. You take them anyhow. Either that or fire a couple of governesses."

In *Sometimes a Great Notion* (1971), an overlooked movie that is one of his best and that he also directed, Newman plays Hank Stamper, a member of a family of rugged individualists headed by Henry Fonda. The Stampers' determination to run the family logging business as they always have done runs smack into the reality of modern times. They refuse to join in a strike against the lumber company that all the loggers sell to, thus weakening the bargaining position of the others. At one point in the movie Willard Eggleston, who owns the local movie theater, tells Hank that the Stampers' truculence is forcing both the other loggers and him into economic ruin, and he threatens suicide. When Hank's wife, Viv (Lee Remick), asks him what he thinks of Willard's plea, he answers casually, "I don't pay much attention to Willard Eggleston. He's in show business."

The Newman family's move away from Hollywood may have seemed to suggest that they didn't pay much attention to people in show business, either. Actually, they only wanted their daily life to be less influenced by it.

"I think I probably care a lot about what people in show business say, but just because I care about it doesn't mean I have to do something about it," he says, starting thoughtfully but ending with a laugh. "I think I avoided most of the traps. What is that marvelous line of Kim's [Stanley] in *Picnic?* She says, 'Darling Alan, I've always liked you.' And he stumbles around. And she says, 'I don't expect you to do anything about it, but I just wanted you to know.'

"I care a lot, obviously. There are a lot of gifted and committed people in motion pictures and they live all over; some of them live in Chicago, some of them live in Hollywood, and I think the trap in Hollywood is that it is really a kind of one intentioned town, and once you get caught up in that swirl [you're swallowed]. Yet there are all of the other things that really can make life exciting. I don't think I would have taken up automobile racing; I don't think I would have gotten immersed in politics in the '60s. It is only when you're away from California that you cannot take yourself seriously; you're allowed the luxury of not taking any of it seriously. Because then you can do something like salad dressing, which is the terminal exploitation, and smile. ..." Here he does. "Well, the slogan of the company is, 'Shameless exploitation in pursuit of the common good.' And that has a kind of rhythm to it that makes sense.

"Joanne has been a big help in that area. I think she figured that out pretty early, too. When we first came to New York, it was really exciting. I'm not a great one for nostalgia but I expect I'm going to be more and more a nut about it, because they were different times. We were treading on new ground and there was a vibrancy about things. And now I think you stay here out of habit and because you've got a lot of friends here."

When Newman was a young actor starting out in New York, he rode around town on a motor scooter because, as he pointed out, it made sense: you got around town much faster. Later he drove a Volkswagen, which was easy to park. But that was a different city, one in which the streets were not war zones and Central Park was safe at any hour and children

**Chance Wayne
(Newman) and Alexandra
del Lago (Geraldine Page)
in the film version of
Sweet Bird of Youth (1962),
a pair of externally
beautiful dreamers whose
souls are a nightmare.**

were unarmed. Even when things got rough, there were boundaries, unlike today. "You could walk home at night," he remembers with a trace of nostalgia. "Joanne could walk home from the theater. I remember fistfights in college where nobody had anything in their pocket. The amazing thing is the acceleration of violence. There are no plateaux."

Apart from moving, 1962 was the year of remakes for Newman. First he reprised his role from *The Battler* in a movie version entitled *Adventures of a Young Man*, and then he and Geraldine Page (her character now named Alexandra del Lago) and almost all of the Broadway cast filmed a clipped-wings version of *Sweet Bird of Youth*, for which Newman was paid $350,000.

There is no mention of syphilis, Chance is beaten up instead of castrated, and as a result of that reparation he is allowed to go with his actress to the supposed glory that awaits them in Hollywood. Still, Williams's intent remains, and Newman is both philosophical and on

target when he says, "You have to make peace with the idea that when you do the motion picture version of the play, it's going to be difficult, and there's no sense struggling with things that were in the play. The character didn't change at all, just the circumstances were different." He calls his performance "pretty good."

Hud (1963) remains one of Newman's defining characters; the part also brought him his third Best Actor Academy Award nomination. The story, from a novel by Larry McMurtry, is a morality play of the highest order; it pits father against son, rectitude against selfishness, and the importance of society against the blind desires of the individual. The conflict is so elemental that it is as if Eugene O'Neill had moved his characters from New England to Texas.

The fulcrum of the piece is, who will set a seventeen-year-old boy (Brandon de Wilde) on his life course? His ageing grandfather, Homer (Melvyn Douglas), a man of principle and integrity who, despite personal devastation, unhesitatingly allows the herd of cattle he has spent his life breeding to be driven into a pit and shot because it is infected with hoof-and-mouth disease? Or his uncle (Newman), a man whose rough charm only occasionally masks his crude arrogance and contempt for others, and whose idea of dealing with the crisis is to sell the animals before tests confirm the suspected infection?

The theme of the movie is struck in one simple exchange of dialogue. Referring to his shooting some buzzards who are waiting to get at the carcass of the calf who has mysteriously died at the beginning of the film, and which are protected by law because they keep the country clean, Hud tells his father, "I always say, the law was meant to be interpreted in a lenient manner, and that's what I do. Sometimes I lean to one side of it, sometimes I lean to the other."

LEFT
When it comes to drinking, fighting, punching cattle, and catching pigs, Hud Bannon is a capable man. When it comes to dealing with people, however, he is more like what he is dragging.

"I don't like to break the law at my place, Hud," Homer calmly answers. And the choice before the boy, as well as the universality of the subject, is summed up by Homer when he says, "Little by little, the look of the country changes because of the men we admire." Hud's opinion: "How many honest men do you know? You take the sinners away from the saints, you're lucky to end up with Abraham Lincoln."

Hud believes that he lost his father's affection fifteen years earlier when he wrecked a car, killing his older brother, and uses that as a subtle excuse for his attitude. But then he is told,

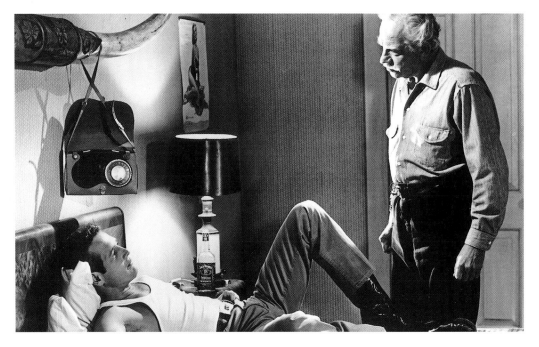

Hud Bannon and his father, Homer (Melvyn Douglas), a man who is as principled as his son is not. "I just naturally had to go bad," Hud tells him, "in the face of so much good." Douglas won an Oscar for Best Supporting Actor.

"No, boy. I was sick of you a long time before that. . . . You don't give a damn. You don't value nothing. . . . You live just for yourself, and that makes you not fit to live with."

"If you don't look out for yourself, the only helping hand you get is when they lower the box," Hud tells his father, and then blames him for how he has turned out. "I just naturally had to go bad, in the face of so much good."

Claiming that his father is no longer capable of handling his own affairs, Hud takes legal action to become guardian of his property. Soon after, his father dies at least in part because of a lost will to live after all his son has done. Hud also drives away the two people who actually care for him. Their attractive and salty housekeeper, Alma (wonderfully played by Patricia Neal), the one woman Hud might have had a decent relationship with—all his involvements in the movie are with married women—leaves because he tries to sexually assault her. And the nephew tells Hud to put his half of the property "in the bank," then goes off to make his own life. (Ten years earlier, in an equally impressive performance, Brandon de Wilde had played Joey, the boy who worships Alan Ladd's doomed ex-gunslinger in another classic Western, *Shane*.) The movie ends with Hud watching him go, then giving a shrugging smile and closing the door.

Newman felt about Hud Bannon the same way he felt about Fast Eddie and Harper that here was a character so rich that he could bring anything to it. When explaining the pleasure of playing a rewarding part he has said, "I come back, always, to *Hud*, because a great many sociological observations were implied in it, in addition to the role itself. To me, *Hud* made the simple statement that people sometimes grow up at tragic expense to other people. It was a wide study of a particular dilemma of our time. I tried to give Hud all the superficial external graces, including the right swing of the body. I took out as many wrinkles as possible. I indicated that he boozed very well, was great with the broads, had a lot of guts, was extraordinarily competent at his job, but had a single tragic flaw: he didn't give a goddam what happened to anyone else. That tragic flaw simply went over everybody's head—especially the reviewers'—and he became a kind of anti-hero, especially among teenagers. One review I'll never forget: it said that *Hud* was quite a marvelous picture. 'The only problem,' the reviewer wrote, 'is that Paul Newman is playing the part, because basically, he has a face that doesn't look lived in.' But Jesus Christ, that's exactly what made the bastard dangerous. The whole *point* of the character is that he has a face that doesn't look lived in. How could he have missed the whole point to such an extraordinary degree? At that exact moment, I realized I should stop reading reviews. And I haven't read one since. Critics don't know what the hell they're talking about, anyway. You get a big fat head if reviews are good and you go into fits of depression if they're bad. Who needs either?"

Hud and Alma (Patricia Neal), the Bannon family housekeeper and the one woman with whom he might have had a decent relationship had he not driven her away. Neal won an Oscar as Best Actress. Newman was nominated but Sidney Poitier won for *Lilies of the Field*.

For all its virtues as a movie, Newman feels that *Hud* "backfired. We thought the last thing people would do was accept Hud as a heroic character. After all, Hud is amoral, greedy, self-centered, selfish, in it for what he can get at the expense of the community. We thought we could give him the external graces ... but morally, he's an empty suit. We thought the audience would be unnerved by that and might be *taught* by that. But kids thought he was terrific! His amorality just went right over their heads; all they saw was this western, heroic individual."

Part of the trouble is that audiences had by then come to expect certain things of a Newman character, and being unrelievedly bad was not one of them. Newman being without redeeming grace is as unconvincing as Clint Eastwood warbling "I Talk to the Trees," which he unfortunately did in *Paint Your Wagon*. Newman knows he can't pull it off.

There comes a point at which an actor reaches a level of stardom where his audience will accept him in only certain kinds of roles, and Newman's combined ability and looks restrained the variety of parts open to him. In Tennessee Williams's plays, he brought a kind of dignity to men difficult to find sympathy for, such as Brick Pollitt, and especially Chance Wayne. Through his thirties and forties and into his fifties, the matinée idol with an attitude suffused his work on film. Whatever the flaws of the character, there was some decency and integrity about Newman that added depth and allowed for kind feelings from the audience; no one wants to leave the theater happy that a Newman character has been punished. He simply isn't a bad guy. His clear vitality and physical allure made it difficult to accept that someone so physically and emotionally attractive could be without *any* saving grace, which helps explain why audiences made Hud an anti-hero instead of the villain he is. But the true rugged individualist in *Hud* is Homer Bannon, the father, who refuses to drill for the oil under his property because unlike cattle, which you tend and breed and chase and sweat over, oil wells require nothing of their owner save that he cash the checks they bring.

Only in the past ten or fifteen years—beginning, perhaps, in 1982 with *The Verdict*, which opens on a hard drinker's face—has age allowed Newman to portray, or rather, allowed the viewer's eye and emotions to accept him in, more brittle parts such as the autocratic General Leslie Groves in *Fat Man and Little Boy*, Walter Bridge in *Mr. and Mrs. Bridge*, and Sully in *Nobody's Fool*. Despite Newman's annoyance with people who mistake the characters for the

man, he admits that he, too, has fallen into that trap. "You get to the point," he says, "where it's much easier to play a role that has been examined and accepted on the screen than it is to play yourself."

Still, that public perception of persona rather than person causes Newman some wonderment. For years he was number one on the male movie-star sex-symbol list. Those blue eyes and that sculpted body helped bring customers into the theaters but, for many, they also obscured the talent underneath them. Newman obviously took his body seriously by working so hard to keep in shape, but he also felt that performance was more important than physique. While in his forties, he explained his dilemma.

"I suppose I should feel flattered, but to think that after *Hud* and *Cool Hand Luke* and all the other pictures I've done and all the parts I've dug into, I come off as the guy women would most like to go to bed with—it's frightening. You break your ass for eighteen years working at your craft and a lady comes up and says, 'Please take off your dark glasses so I can see your blue eyes.' If I died today, they might write on my tombstone, 'Here lies Paul Newman, died at age forty-three, a failure because his eyes turned brown.' It's really awful. I'd like to think there's a mind functioning somewhere in Paul Newman, and a soul, and a political conscience, and a talent that extends beyond the blueness of my eyes—and my capacity for bedroom gymnastics. ... Take Joanne in *Rachel, Rachel*. Study that virginal face and the tightly controlled smile and the pinched way in which she carries her body. It's got nothing to do with the lady when she gets home and takes off her makeup. The same is true with me." (Once at a charity event where he was ladling punch, an adoring woman asked him to stir her cup with his finger. "I'd be glad to," he told her, "but I just took it out of a cyanide bottle.")

Several years ago he told Maureen Dowd of *The New York Times* a story that he hoped would reveal the real Paul Newman's reaction to someone dealing with Paul Newman the sex symbol. He was walking along Fifth Avenue when he saw a woman in a white dress who was causing a stir. "A real stunner," he said. "Man, drivers were jumping the curb to get a better look." Newman and the woman caught each other's eye in a moment of mutual appreciation as they passed, and he continued on his way. A couple of blocks later he stopped to look into the window of an antiques shop, and he felt a tap on his shoulder. It was the woman in white, who explained that she was a call girl but that it would be a pleasure to be with him for free. He paused, and paused some more. He was blushing.

"You think about how you would play a moment like that," he said. "You want to send her off with something classy and stylish, the way Cary Grant would, or Clint Eastwood. You think, how would Hombre handle this?

"And when this woman came up to me—the guy who played Hud—what comes through? Laurel and Hardy. Both of them. All I could manage was this massive foot shuffling and dancing around, like a worm on the end of a hook. I was still shuffling," he said, grinning, "eight blocks later."

Here's why: "If you don't have a chance to rehearse," he says, "you're not a sex symbol."

After *Hud*, Newman had five movies open in quick succession—*A New Kind of Love*, *The Prize*, *The Outrage*, *What a Way to Go!*, and *Lady L*. He was now free of studio constraints and wanted to build creative and financial stability by working in partnership with people he admired and trusted. He and director Martin Ritt formed an alliance known as Jodell Productions, taking its name from their wives, Joanne and Adele; and he established the Newman-Foreman Company with John Foreman, his and Woodward's former agent. Through these companies he hoped to establish himself as a producer and expand his range of characters, as well as provide chances for collaborations with his wife.

A New Kind of Love is a broad romantic comedy that just never gelled. In the right kind of script—*Slap Shot*, for example—Newman is a very good comedian. But as audiences saw in *Rally Round the Flag, Boys!* (1958), or *Lady L* (1965), farce is not a Newman strength. Even so, he gamely tried to master the genre, and to please Woodward as well.

"Joanne read it and said, 'Hey, this would be fun to do together. Read it.' I read it and said, 'Joanne, it's just a bunch of one-liners.' And she said, 'You son of a bitch, I've been carting your children around, taking care of them at the expense of my career, taking care of you and your house.' And I said, 'That's what I said. It's a terrific script. I can't think of anything I'd rather do.' This is what is known as a reciprocal trade agreement."

The Prize, a Hitchcockesque thriller written by Ernest Lehman, who wrote *North By Northwest*, featured Newman as a drunken novelist who ends up solving the mystery of a

At home with Clea, born in 1965, their third child and third daughter. Newman had three children from his first marriage.

Nobel scientist's kidnapping and replacement by a look-alike (Edward G. Robinson). The story is entirely implausible but Newman is amusing.

The Outrage, a reworking of Akira Kurosawa's *Rashomon*, was moved from medieval Japan to modern Mexico. Each witness to a rape and murder has a different account of what occurred. Newman at first turned down the part, suggesting Marlon Brando as better for it. But when Brando, who wanted to take it on, couldn't because of other commitments, Newman relented. "I liked that one," he says of the movie, perhaps in part because his usual looks had an overlay of dirt, whiskers and matted hair, and he thus forced the audience to consider him solely as an actor.

But he adds, "I'm not so sure that *The Outrage* works. Those chances when I have been able to forage farthest afield I guess are the parts I like the most. I don't know how well I did. I've never been comfortable watching a movie of mine. There's always something that strikes me as being pushed or demonstrated or phony, or something that rubs me the wrong way."

In the midst of this spate of movies, Newman and Woodward did a four-month run off Broadway in *Baby Want a Kiss*, written by their friend and former beau of Woodward, James Costigan, and produced by the Actors Studio. It was a beneficial move for the pair of actors; Newman's recent movies had not been smashes and Woodward's career had idled. This was an opportunity for them to do something they did very well and to do it together. It was even more beneficial to the Actors Studio, which reaped the benefits of sold-out houses every night. Newman and Woodward took only the Actor's Equity minimum salary of $107.50 a week.

The play was Newman's artistic highlight for the next year or so, although 1965 was personally brightened by the birth of his and Joanne's third daughter, Clea. There is not much good to say about two pieces of slapstick, *What a Way to Go!* (1964), in which he was one of several husbands of Shirley MacLaine who start poor, become rich, and then die in ironic ways— he was a French painter who is devoured by the painting machine he has invented— and *Lady L* (1965), in which he is the determined anarchist lover of Sophia Loren. "I woke up every morning and knew I wasn't cutting the mustard," he says.

But *Harper* (1966) is another matter.

The movie was his first for Warner Bros. since he had bought out his contract, and it had to be sweet going back. In one swoop he would avenge the days when the studio made $75,000 per movie from loan-out fees while he was paid $17,500. For this movie he would receive $750,000 plus 10 percent of the gross after $7.5 million, whether the cost of making the movie was recouped or not. It was an even better deal for producers Jerry Gershwin and Elliott Kastner, whose gross percentage kicked in at either $7.5 million or two and a half times the cost of the negative, whichever was higher. Newman was clearly in charge, and he pushed for the movie to be made in color rather than the planned black and white.

Perhaps in an act of conciliation, or maybe because he was forced to acknowledge Newman's power, Jack Warner came down to see him during the first week of rehearsals.

"How are ya?" Warner asked, then reached into his coat pocket. "You smoke cigars?"

"No," Newman answered, "I only smoke people, Jack. You know that."

Warner laughed and photographers took pictures of them smiling together. For a subsequent Christmas Newman sent out a special greetings card to people who knew both of them, and also sent one to Warner. On the front was the traditional "Peace on Earth." Inside was the picture of Warner and Newman smiling and the antecedent, "Good Will Toward Men." Those in the know had a great laugh at the irony, Warner included.

"What an extraordinary man," Newman said not long after *Harper* was released. "I've never known a greater vulgarian—not even Khruschev; he calls my wife 'Joan.' On second thought … he's only the second greatest. The champ happens to be another Hollywood mogul, but he'll have to remain nameless."

The ads for the picture mimicked a reading primer:

This is Harper's gun.

See how black and shiny it is.

It is Harper's very best friend.

See how much Harper needs his friend.

See *Harper*.

That was appropriate in a way, because the movie was a return to the beginning of the genre. *Harper* excised twenty-five years of mutant growth for the American private eye. He began with Humphrey Bogart, first as Sam Spade in *The Maltese Falcon* (1941). As the critic

With Jack Warner—"the second greatest vulgarian I've known"—shortly after returning to Warner Bros. in 1966 for the first time since he had bought out his contract seven years earlier. The picture was taken during rehearsals for *Harper*. Despite the momentary smile, the two never got along, and Newman had the photo made into a Christmas card with the ironic greeting, "Good Will Toward Men."

Judith Crist wrote when *Harper* came out, "He existed relatively intact through the '40s, most often as Philip Marlowe, created by Bogart for *The Big Sleep* (1946) and re-created by Dick Powell, Robert Montgomery and George Montgomery for such films as *Murder, My Sweet*; *Lady in the Lake*; and *The Brasher Doubloon*. Then, during the '50s and on into the '60s, with the global and sexual and sensational reorientation of movies, he underwent a heady transformation—until he was lost completely to the Bonds and the Matt Helms, the *Dragnet* robots and the agents from U.N.C.L.E. ... Men they were not. Symbols, yes—men, no." These new heroes were cartoons. "At best they may find a lip-service kind of job loyalty that permits the symbol to deal out death, at worst with indifference, and at most times to undergo assaults and torture as if he had been a favorite tutee of von Sacher-Masoch." With Spades and Marlowes, however, "When they got hit they hurt and they needed time to recover; when they killed they flinched and were gnawed by regret. Above all, they did what they had to because they were men, in the head and the heart and not exclusively in the groin."

Lew Harper was the reincarnation of that. He slept in his office, had to use yesterday's coffee grounds to brew this morning's jolt, and loved his wife even though she had thrown him out of the house and was doing her best to divorce him. The only difference between Spade and Harper comes in one of the many wonderful exchanges in William Goldman's screenplay from Ross Macdonald's novel, *The Moving Target*. For instance, this one with Lauren Bacall. That she is Bogart's widow makes it even better:

"Like a drink?"

"Not before lunch."

"I thought you were a detective."

"New type."

Bacall played Mrs. Sampson, the much younger wife of a missing millionaire whom

In *Harper* (1966), a character he modeled in part on Robert F. Kennedy. "If you didn't watch him closely, you'd think he wasn't listening. It's not that there isn't contact; he's really honed in and sharp ... [but] it kind of puts you off until you get used to it. I thought it was a nice bit of business for a private detective."

Harper is brought in to find, not that it matters much to her:

"I only want to outlive him. I want to see him in his grave."

Then with no remorse. "What a terrible thing to say."

"People in love will say anything," Harper answers laconically.

Much fun is had at the expense of Los Angeles, such as when Harper says, "Your husband keeps lousy company, Mrs. Sampson, as bad as there is in L.A. And that's as bad as there is."

Harper does his best to keep an ongoing relationship with his would-be ex-wife, Susan, played by Janet Leigh. He always shows up at her house when he's in trouble. On one occasion, he has been badly beaten up and looks it. She finally lets him in the house and he soon has his arms around her.

"What do you want from me?" she asks.

"A few kind words."

"Anything else?"

"Anything I can get."

In something of a rarity for him at the time, Newman did not hang out with private eyes or wander the streets of Los Angeles in preparation for the role. Rather, he says, he formulated much of his characterization during a transatlantic plane flight.

Before *Hud* and *The Outrage*, "I sniffed around [the location], found out as much about the character and the locale as I could. But with *Harper* I simply got drunk. I had read the script a few times, and I was flying from Liverpool to New York when I started reading it again. I made certain specific … notes, like 'Funnier line here,' or 'What does his car look like?' [it's a beat-up Porsche] … and 'chewing gum' and 'do it detached.'"

Harper is hard-boiled and stylish, as well as witty and well plotted. The dialogue relies on real language rather than expletives, and the audience gets the clues as they come to Harper—who chews a lot of gum—rather than by any gimmicks. There is little blood (although Harper's abrasions from a run-in with two thugs look very real) and by any comparison with today's movies, scarce violence. A scene toward the end where the bad guys extract information from Julie Harris is bloodcurdling not for what we see but for the screams that we hear while the camera is busy showing Harper's arrival. Which makes the letter written to Jack Warner by Geoffrey M. Shurlock, a censor with the Motion Picture Association of America Production Code office, all the more stunning for what it shows has happened to movies in the past thirty years.

Harper, Shurlock cautioned Warner, "contains objectionable elements of savagery which would render your finished picture unacceptable under the requirements of the Code. … The word Hell is used to excess throughout the script. If we are to approve your finished picture, there should be a drastic reduction of the number of occasions where the expression is used. … Also 'Like Hell' and 'What the hell' … [the phrase] 'Old bag of worms' seems unacceptably vulgar.'"

The Alfred Hitchcock movie *Torn Curtain* (1966) followed, in which Newman plays an American nuclear scientist who wangles his way to picking the brain of a famous East German scientist by pretending to be a defector. Nothing in the movie works. It looked as if his career had fallen back again. Actually, it was just a slight misstep before it entered one of its best periods.

Cool Hand Luke (1967) begins as a conventional picture about a guy a little too unheeding of authority, who is sent to chain-gang camp for a dumb act—in this case, knocking the heads off parking meters to get the change—and whose already miserable life spirals downward from there. Yet, very quickly, Luke goes from being a dunce who brings on his own troubles to a victim of not only the brutish prison system and its sadistic warders, but also of the adulation of the other prisoners, who begin by ridiculing him but come to idolize his almost existential defiance. For the first time in his life, Luke has respect. Unfortunately, his pleasure in his elevation contributes to his death, because he believes he is as indestructible as do his mates.

Everyone remembers the funny scene in which Luke wins a wager by eating fifty hard-boiled eggs. But what helps make the movie so poignant and powerful is the scene in which Luke's mother (Jo Van Fleet) comes to visit him propped up in the back of a truck. Through her we come to see his background and the root of the hamstrung emotions of this loner whose destiny is to lose. Newman received his fourth Best Actor Academy Award nomination for playing Luke, and for the fourth time did not win. Rather than sulk, he expanded his career.

While acting on Broadway in *Sweet Bird of Youth* in 1959 Newman directed the actor Michael Strong in a twenty-eight-minute movie version of Chekhov's monologue *The Harmful Effects of Tobacco*, a piece of work that in 1966 he called "the best creative experience I've ever had. I was just absolutely alive. My wife must have thought I was on dope." When asked about it now a pleasant look crosses Newman's face as he says, "That's the first time that film has passed through my consciousness in twenty-five years. It's very clumsy, but the piece itself is wonderful."

Rachel, Rachel (1968), on the other hand, has stayed with him. It was the first feature he directed. ("Actors want to direct because they get fed up with the restriction of acting inside their own skin," he says.) He was also the producer through Kayos Productions (pronounced "chaos"), part of the Newman-Foreman Company. His partner, John Foreman, had seen a review of *A Jest of God* by the Canadian writer Margaret Laurence and got the galleys of her novel about a thirty-five-year-old spinster schoolteacher with an outwardly bland but emotionally colorful life. He and Woodward read and then optioned it, even though Newman was not impressed at first. "Not movie material," she quoted him as saying. Foreman and

Woodward continued with it, hiring family friend Stewart Stern, who had written the screenplay for *Rebel Without a Cause* and *The Ugly American* as well as *The Rack*, and who had been helpful with polishing *The Young Philadelphians*, to work on the script.

"I went around offering ourselves to everybody," Woodward told Rex Reed in *The New York Times*, "but I'm afraid offering a package of the script and me was hardly like offering Elizabeth Taylor and Tennessee Williams."

Even Newman adding his name to the project as director did little to impress the big studios. After many rejections Warner Bros.-Seven Arts committed $700,000 to it with the

After *Cool Hand Luke* ate fifty hard-boiled eggs, contests to outdo him spread throughout college campuses and among the troops in Vietnam.

common proviso that Newman pay for any overrun. Where they got their pound of flesh was making him also agree to act in two movies for them at half his regular price, and for Joanne Woodward to do one.

"I got involved in it about the same way the United States got involved in the Vietnam War," Newman told Michael Billington of *The Times* of London. "I came in as an adviser and found the whole process had escalated until I was directing. ... I had some ideas about the book and the structuring of it and there were a few conflicting discussions between myself and the writer, Stewart Stern, until I gradually realized I just had to direct it. It was the only way to settle the conflicts we were having! But [my directing a movie] would have happened sooner or later anyway. ..."

There also was the sense of a challenge to do something many thought he could not. He was determined, he said to Rex Reed, not only to show that he could direct but also "to prove to Hollywood you can make a film about basic, simple people, without violence and a band of Indians scalping the settlers."

"I'm not a particularly vindictive man," he added to Billington, "but I must say I now read the letters of rejection I got for the film with a certain quiet pleasure. There is, shall we say, a good deal of inward chuckling."

The movie was something of a family affair. Besides Woodward and their friend Stern, their daughter Nell, who has her father's eyes but otherwise has her mother's looks, played Rachel as a little girl. "As a parent I was against that, but as a director I thought she was great," Newman says. Also in the cast were Frank Corsaro, who had directed the Newmans in *Baby Want a Kiss* off-Broadway, and Newman's auto mechanic, Bruno Engel. His brother, Arthur, was associate producer, and Dede Allen, the unparalleled movie editor who worked on *The Hustler*, was on the set daily to advise Newman on how shots should be made so that they would piece together to best effect. "I don't understand those directors who want to cut their own pictures all the time," he told Billington.

While the original thought had been to shoot the movie in California, a studio was built inside a gymnasium in Danbury, Connecticut, because, "I very much wanted to contrast the schoolteacher's rather arid, dry existence with the lush, verdant spring background—it would have been far too obvious to have placed a barren life against a barren setting."

With Joanne Woodward making *Rachel, Rachel* (1968), the first film Newman directed.

Woodward portrays a spinster schoolteacher who lives with and takes care of her sickly but domineering mother in their apartment over a funeral home. In that summer of her thirty-fifth year she realizes that life is about to leave her behind for good and so sets out to overcome her frustration and boredom, and the claustrophobia of her small town, before it is too late. She loses her virginity—or rather, she eagerly gives it away—to a former high school friend who's come home for a visit, and thinks that love and marriage will follow. When they don't but a presumed pregnancy does, she makes plans to move to Oregon. In the end the pregnancy turns out to be a cyst—the jest of God—but she now has the impetus to leave and the hope that life can be different.

Newman wanted the movie to look as uncomplicated as possible, so although he used many flashbacks and fantasies, he told Billington that he didn't want the movie to appear "tricky. The function of the camera was simply to eavesdrop. I made it a rule that the actor would never go to the camera: the camera would always come to him. It was rather like the old days of television." A couple of years later he added to critic Roger Ebert: "There's a con-spiracy against the actor in this town … on every level. You get these technically oriented sets and every shot is set up for the convenience of the technicians. And you get your motor running and have to stop while they move around some lights or rub a piece of tissue across your nose. Aargh!"

"In directing Joanne," he told *Life*, "I used what we call the active verb. It's terribly aca-demic, but if you can find an active verb to describe the scene, you can always give the actor the right direction. If you tell an actress to 'pinch it'—which is what I kept digging away at Joanne about—she'll suck that sensation into her body and you're going to get a certain physical quality from her. Her laughter becomes pinched and a bit self-conscious; her mouth becomes pursed, her reactions become crimped. An actress as good as Joanne will even turn in her toes."

The reporter Gene Wilson described their working together as "almost totally physical, so that their communications sometimes suggested those of two deaf-mutes. He put the palms of his hands on her cheeks, bent forward and peered into her eyes, snarled at her, and then moved his hands to the back of her neck and pushed her head slowly from side to side. When he stopped, she nodded in strong agreement. He went and sat down on a box to rest before the next take, and without speaking she began to massage his neck and shoulders, occasionally bending his head forward sharply and then jerking it back again by the hair."

Newman found directing was not nearly so tiring as acting. "As an actor," he told Joan Barthel of *The New York Times*, "you stop and start the motor all day; it's like running 100 yards two feet at a time." But when one is involved with every aspect of film there is no time to slow down. What Newman enjoyed most was what he calls "the intellect of making films." With that in mind, he told Barthel, his perfect movie would go like this:

"You get a marvelous, original idea for a picture. Then you get a playwright and you start working on developing a first draft. Then you start developing a second draft. Then you start thinking in terms of casting and locations, then you work more on the production, more on the casting, then you actually cast. Then you set up the production and you start your rehearsal with the actors. You rehearse diligently and marvelously and you make all kinds of discoveries about the actors, about the nature of the manuscript, what changes are needed, what works, what doesn't work, what you need in terms of additional dialogue and new scenes. Then you rehearse for two weeks—you figure out your entire production team, the lights and the sound and so forth—and you work with the set designer and you go through all that.

"You finish your last day of rehearsal on a Friday afternoon at 5:30, then you say WRAP, and everyone goes home, and you never shoot a foot of film."

Such was not the case with *Rachel, Rachel,* and even Newman had to be glad. The movie did $8 million worth of business and he and Woodward each received excellent reviews of their work. "The best written, most seriously acted American movie in a long time ... Miss Woodward [is] extraordinarily good. ... If this were a less ironic age, it might [be] like a kind of American cinema Balzac," wrote Renata Adler in *The New York Times.* Richard Schickel added in *Life* that "Newman is anything but the bouncing boy-o we are accustomed to seeing on our screens. He has a sensitive, slightly melancholic eye for something most American movies miss—the texture of ordinary life. He displays, moreover, a feel for emotional nuance and a technical sureness; he is neither too radical nor too conservative. This is remarkable in a first movie."

The Academy of Motion Picture Arts and Sciences agreed, giving the movie four Oscar nominations, including three of the five biggest: for picture, screenplay, and actress (Woodward). Newman won the New York Film Critics Circle Award for directing, Woodward for Best Actress.

Newman closed out a decade in which he would release twenty movies very productively, with the exception of *The Secret War of Harry Frigg*, his first movie after *Rachel, Rachel. Harry* was intended to be a comedy about a loser of an Army private whose sole talent seems to be escaping from the stockade. The title alone, a sophomoric attempt at winkingly risqué language, gives a hint of what's to come.

"As Private Harry," Renata Adler wrote, "Newman is supposed to be slope-shouldered, floppy and comic. ... He sits, in a ragdoll way, on a prison truck and fakes a yawn; and the part won't bend. The scene becomes a charade in which Paul Newman is trying to communicate that he is not playing Hud this time: and what we have here, as Cool Hand Luke would say, is a failure to communicate."

But then in rode Robert Leroy Parker and Harry Longbaugh, better known as Butch Cassidy and the Sundance Kid, and all was forgiven from the moment at the start of the movie when Butch walks in to case a bank that he and the Kid have robbed before. Bars are in the windows, a big safe is being installed, and there is now a guard, whom Butch asks what happened to the nice old bank that obviously had no security at all. Too many robberies, he tells Cassidy, who answers indignantly, "That's a small price to pay for beauty!"

Butch Cassidy and the Sundance Kid (1969) makes the Old West as romantic as the Sherwood Forest of Robin Hood, and equally as unrealistic. Never mind, the movie is celestial cotton candy. Butch, the leader of the Hole in the Wall Gang, and Sundance (Robert Redford) are committed to the notion of robbing from the rich to give to the poor, in this case themselves. But they're very good-natured about it. Butch is perfectly willing to have Mr. E. H. Harriman of the Union Pacific Railway (as he's generally referred to) just give Sundance and him what Harriman takes to spending on security to foil them, and he'll leave the trains alone. But the pair discovers that railway barons take poorly to pesky robbers and are willing to spend a great deal to put them in their place, if only out of pride. All of which mystifies Butch and the Kid. After all, they've never really hurt anybody. It's not until they

Newman and Woodward in 1969 after receiving the New York Film Critics Circle Awards for Best Director and Best Actress for their work in *Rachel, Rachel*. Woodward was also nominated for an Academy Award.

flee to Bolivia to escape Harriman's vigilantes and try to go straight that they actually shoot at someone—ironically, would-be robbers of a shipment of gold that they've actually been hired to guard.

Etta Place (Katharine Ross) is the presumed object of affection. She and the Kid are an item, but the love scene is between Butch and her. After he has ridden her around the meadow on a bicycle to the tune of "Raindrops Keep Falling on My Head," she asks him whether things would be different if the two of them had met first. "We're involved, Etta; don't you know that?" he replies. "I mean, you're riding on my bicycle—in certain Arabian countries that's the same as being married." Butch also performs impressive handlebar acrobatics, such as standing on the seat on one leg with the other straight out behind. These were supposed to be done by a stunt double, who complained that they were too dangerous. So Newman did them. The scene was an addition by the director, George Roy Hill, who decided midway through shooting that there needed to be a relationship between Butch and Etta. But despite the beautiful woman, the movie is really a love story between two guys who are being squeezed to death by the increasingly tame New West.

As Harriman's posse closes in, the gang disperses and Butch and Sundance hide out at Etta's. They plan to go it alone until the Kid suggests that she come along. A woman would be good cover, he reasons, because no one would expect them to be with one; it would make for safer travel. That decided, he turns to Etta and tells her, "What I'm saying is, if you want to go, I won't stop you. But the minute you start to whine or make a nuisance, I don't care where we are, I'm dumping you."

"Don't sugarcoat it like that, Kid," Butch interrupts. "Tell her straight."

Etta, who turns out to be a reliable extra gun as well as a capable cook, responds with a gravity found only in the recently adolescent: "I'm twenty-six and I'm single and I teach school and that's the bottom of the pit. And the only excitement I've ever known is here with me now. So I'll go with you, and I won't whine, and I'll sew your socks and I'll stitch you when you're wounded, and anything you ask of me I'll do except one thing: I won't watch you die. I'll miss that scene, if you don't mind."

Etta is as good as her word. She sees the end coming before the audience and the finale is left to Butch and Sundance, who become the scourge of the Bolivian banking system and

Preparing the bicycle for Newman's stunts in *Butch Cassidy and the Sundance Kid* **(1969). Katharine Ross is on the right.**

attract the attention of what seems the entire army. They are spotted just as they settle down to lunch at an outdoor cantina in a small town from whose bank they intend to make a withdrawal. After a hail of bullets hits everything at the table except them, Butch declares with his usual calm directness, "That settles it. This place gets no more of my business."

Surrounded and wounded, they fight on, short on bullets, maybe, but long on *bons mots*. When the Kid says he's going to run outside to get a better angle and asks for cover, Butch answers, "This is no time for bravery: I'll let you."

Later, as hundreds of soldiers pump bullets into the building they're holed up in and both of them bleed heavily from their wounds, Butch has a brainstorm for where they should go next.

"Australia."

Sundance is nonplussed. "Australia! That's your idea?"

Butch nods sagely. "The latest in a long line."

They get no farther than the street outside, where in freeze frame they are left standing as the fusillade from hundreds of guns echoes.

"Too bad they got killed at the end," Newman says, " 'cause those two guys could have gone on in films forever."

In a way they do go on, as trademarks of Newman's and Redford's favorite charitable institutions. Redford has named his movie workshop the Sundance Institute, while Newman's camp for children with leukemia and other diseases of the blood is called the Hole in the Wall Gang Camp. The irony is that Redford, who is so indelibly identified with the Sundance Kid, was the fourth choice to play the part. First it was to be a Newman-Brando picture with Newman as the Kid, but Brando was too involved with social causes to act. Then the plan was for Newman and Warren Beatty, with Newman as Butch. When that didn't work out, Steve McQueen was slotted for the Kid. Only after that failed did Redford come in. Just as Humphrey Bogart got the parts in *The Maltese Falcon* and *Casablanca* because George Raft misguidedly dropped out, and Newman scored in movies meant for James Dean, Redford gained one of his most recognizable roles simply by being there at the end of the dance, and he won a British Film Academy Award for Best Actor.

The ads for the film played on the physical assets of the stars, most dramatically in a black and white poster with two pairs of very blue eyes shining out. It signalled not only their great looks but also a sense that an old movie form had a modern look. And just as the movie put a contemporary spin on two characters whose time had passed, *Butch Cassidy and the Sundance Kid* was itself something of an end of an era for Newman.

Movie heroes (or anti-heroes) have a comparatively short life expectancy before they mutate into someone more relative to current culture. John Wayne eventually turned into Butch Cassidy; *Casablanca*'s Rick Blaine became Cool Hand Luke. In turn, the characters that Newman and other actors played with such success in the '60s transmogrified. First they became more nihilist, then cartoonish as the darker than life *Taxi Driver* developed into the bigger than life *Terminator*.

Fifteen years into his movie career, it was time for Newman to make some changes, too.

Paul Newman
as himself.

In car-racing gear. "I can't be competitive about acting, because there's no way to compete as an actor. What are you competing against? In auto racing, either you win or you lose. You go across the finish line and come in first or second or ninth—or not at all."

BELOW

Campaigning for Eugene McCarthy in 1968. Newman presented himself to audiences not as a celebrity but as a parent, concerned about the future. "I don't want it written on my gravestone, 'He was not part of his times.' The times are too critical to be dissenting in your own bathroom."

ABOVE
Father and daughters, c. 1975.

RIGHT
At the auto racetrack with daughter, Melissa, c. 1974–5.

**At the Le Mans 24-hour race,
1979. His team finished second.**

ABOVE
With Joanne Woodward at their home in Connecticut.

LEFT
Between shots while filming *Harry and Son* (1984).

FAR LEFT
Poster for *Buffalo Bill and the Indians, or Sitting Bull's History Lesson* (1976).

Newman, here during the making of *Harry and Son*, has a reputation for being a very focused director.

LEFT
Col. "Pops" Newman promoting Newman's Own popcorn. His "Shameless exploitation in pursuit of the common good," as the company slogan goes, has so far benefitted nearly 400 charitable organizations around the world.

ABOVE
**Between takes during the making
of *Mr. and Mrs. Bridge* (1990).**

RIGHT
**As Donald "Sully" Sullivan in
Nobody's Fool (1994).**

Newman risked his enormous popularity to campaign vigorously for Senator Eugene McCarthy, who opposed the Vietnam War; he started First Artists, a production and distribution company in partnership with Barbra Streisand and Sidney Poitier; and he took up auto racing. The first two were valiant efforts that failed. The third was another matter.

In backing McCarthy he was not a political neophyte endorsing the candidate of the moment. He had stuffed envelopes for the presidential campaigns of Senator Adlai Stevenson, who was twice beaten by Dwight Eisenhower in the 1950s; contributed to the Democratic Party and to civil rights causes; and stumped for his friend Gore Vidal when Vidal ran for Congress in Upstate New York in 1965 against a conservative Republican incumbent. Newman's fame helped bring out crowds for Vidal; he says 1,400 showed up for a rally at which he and Woodward were featured, but the local press carried "a story on page nine—two inches long. It didn't mention that I was there or that Joanne or anybody else was there. It didn't even mention Gore's name. It just said 'the Democratic candidate' spoke."

It was different with McCarthy. The 1968 presidential election was one of the most passionate in United States history, and it was McCarthy's strong showing against the President from his own party in the New Hampshire primary election in March that convinced Lyndon Johnson not to seek another term. In June, Senator Robert F. Kennedy would be murdered while campaigning in Los Angeles. Newman was one of the earliest backers of McCarthy, and his support came at a time when most people considered those who opposed the war to be cowards or even traitors. Newman's appearance always brought out the news media. He presented himself to audiences not as a celebrity but as a parent, concerned about the future and believing that McCarthy offered the most hope.

"I am indifferent to your political persuasion," he would begin. "I am not a public speaker. I am not a politician. I'm not here because I'm an actor. I'm here because I've got six kids. I don't want it written on my gravestone, 'He was not part of his times.' The times are too critical to be dissenting in your own bathroom."

Another politician besides McCarthy plied the voters of New Hampshire. Richard Nixon, who was as conservative as Newman is liberal and who was sometimes referred to as Tricky Dick, followed Newman on one swing through the state. An automobile dealer had loaned Newman a brand-new Jaguar for three days, and Newman discovered when he returned it that it would next be loaned to Nixon. Always happy to play a practical joke, he left a note on the dashboard: "Dear Mr. Nixon: You should have no trouble driving this car at all, because it has a very tricky clutch."

In 1973, when then President Richard Nixon's enemies list was published, Newman was high on it, and he attributes his inclusion as much to the note as to any of his activities. "I have been fortunate in my lifetime to be tapped for a reasonable abundance of honors," he says, "but none delighted me or elevated me in the eyes of my children more than my placement as number nineteen on Mr. Nixon's enemies list. I do not anticipate encomium of similar consequence, but then, hope springs eternal."

Newman and the playwright Arthur Miller were two of the delegates from Connecticut for McCarthy at the Democratic National Convention in Chicago in August 1968, and Newman's opposition to the war continued. In October 1969 he and Joanne Woodward were among more than 200 protestors in an antiwar demonstration in front of the American Embassy in London's Grosvenor Square. Later that year he and other stars urged a boycott of movies they were in as an antiwar protest, despite owning a percentage of the profits.

In *WUSA* (1970) Newman tried to put his activism and political beliefs into his work. He played an alienated drifter who lands a job as a disc jockey for an ultraconservative New Orleans radio station, and who slowly discovers a right-wing political plot. He calls the result "a film of incredible potential, which the producer, the director and I loused up. We tried to make it political, and it wasn't."

Newman refuses to concern himself with how his political beliefs are interpreted. "People in Hollywood come up to me and say, 'Why take a chance? Don't make enemies,'" he says. "My reaction is, 'Kiss off.' I still have my citizenship papers. Did I lose them when I became an actor? What they're basically asking me to do is be a person without character. A person without character has no enemies. So I prefer to make enemies."

He backed his public support with financial donations. In the 1960s he established the No Sutch Foundation to channel some of his earnings to groups whose work he wanted to support. In 1965, for example, he gave away about $100,000, most of it to black civil rights organizations. In 1970 he narrated the award-winning documentary *King: A Filmed Record … Montgomery to Memphis*, directed by Joseph L. Mankiewicz and Sidney Lumet.

His public involvement in political affairs continued throughout the 1970s, and letters to the editor of *The New York Times* on such issues as environmental protection, Arab terrorists, Big Oil, civil rights and nuclear arms limitations were published. In 1978 he was one of five representatives designated by President Jimmy Carter to attend a United Nations General Assembly session on disarmament, an issue he remained deeply involved with publicly through the 1980s. (He has described nuclear warheads as "the great relaxers in the sky.")

In June 1969 Newman, Barbra Streisand, and Sidney Poitier formed First Artists Production Company to finance, arrange distribution of and control all facets of the movies they made. Before long they were joined by Steve McQueen and Dustin Hoffman. Each star agreed to make at least three pictures. Just as Mary Pickford, Douglas Fairbanks, Charlie Chaplin and D. W. Griffith had done fifty years earlier in forming United Artists, the actors hoped that greater control would make for both better movies and higher profits.

It didn't work out that way. In the slightly more than ten years the company was in business there were some notable hits—McQueen's *The Getaway*, for instance—but for the most part the stars and the company made poor choices, McQueen's case being a fine example. His second movie was a version of the 1882 Henrik Ibsen play *An Enemy of the People*, for which he fattened himself up to 200 pounds and further obscured his looks beneath a beard. Its very limited release did not come until 1977, but it is better than most of his final films. First Artists threatened to sue him for failure to meet his obligations to the company and virtually forced him to make the disastrous western *Tom Horn* (1980).

Newman's three movies were a mixed bag. In *Pocket Money* (1972) he was Jim Kane, a hard-luck, modern-day cowboy much like a more comic Cool Hand Luke. *The Drowning Pool* (1976) was an unsuccessful sequel to *Harper*. *The Life and Times of Judge Roy Bean* (1972), an update of the 1940 classic *The Westerner* with Gary Cooper and Walter Brennan, was the best of the lot. Newman's performance as the judge, the self-proclaimed law west of the Pecos, is often hilarious. Jim Kane and Roy Bean are broadly comic, and two of Newman's more interesting characters. He lists them among his favorites.

Newman entered into the deal to form First Artists just at the time when auto racing pulled away his interest from acting. He had always liked automobiles and fooling around with them. When living in Beverly Hills he drove a Volkswagen, in part to thumb his nose at

With Ava Gardner as the actress Lily Langtry in *The Life and Times of Judge Roy Bean* (1972). Newman's portrayal of the judge, the self-proclaimed law west of the Pecos, is broadly comic and often hilarious.

the culture of fancy automobiles that perpetually grips Los Angeles, although his 1963 Volkswagen *did* have a Porsche engine and transmission and other high-performance equipment. One night Newman and Woodward drove in it to a black-tie gala for Britain's Princess Margaret. Afterwards several hundred party-goers who were waiting for their automobiles to be brought around applauded when Newman and Woodward climbed into their Beetle and peeled away.

He also had a passion for motorcycles. The Lambretta scooter he used in Manhattan was really just for maneuvering in traffic. When he lived in Beverly Hills his three motorcycles were a means of escape. "Sometimes you need to relieve the pressure," he said in 1966. "Having that old brute bike on the front porch and driving it to the beach after dinner is just marvelous. Within minutes you're looser."

Racing driver P. L. Newman at the Riverside International Race Track in the early 1970s, shortly after he took up the sport.

To the great relief of studio executives who worried about him hurting himself and stalling productions, he sold the cycles after a 1965 accident in which his blue Triumph hit a slick spot on Sunset Boulevard and skidded out of control. The bike required $24 worth of repairs. Newman's were more costly. He had third-degree burns on both legs and scrapes on several fingers that required skin grafts.

Newman's pleasure in motored things was not dampened by the accident, and it made *Winning* (1969) an attractive script for him. It is both a relationship and an action drama, with footage of the 1967 Indianapolis 500 interspersed in the story. The relationship centers around Newman, a race auto driver, Woodward, the mother of a teenage boy (Richard Thomas), and Robert Wagner, Newman's friend and competitor. Among the twists are Newman's evolving involvement with the boy, the rise and fall and rise again of his love affair with Woodward, and a pivotal scene in which he finds her in bed with Wagner. "Ha!" Woodward said to Rex Reed in *The New York Times*, alluding to roles associated with all three lead actors. "We're calling it *Cool Hand Luke Finds Rachel in the Sack with the Saint!*"

It was while filming *Winning* that racing captivated him. He started off driving around pylons in a parking lot and then the terrier in him took over. He found he not only liked racing, but that with hard work it was something he learned to do better and better, until quite literally he became as good a driver as he is an actor. He claims he is a terrible dancer, an awful tennis player, and a "suicide-crouch" skier, but that racing makes him feel graceful.

"I just decided one day, why *not* do it?" he says. "It's marvelous to say, 'I want to do it because I think it's going to be fun.' Then you surprise yourself when you do it because it *is* fun. It's just fun; that's all." It is also such a sharp contrast to acting, which is an entirely subjective undertaking. "I can't be competitive about acting, because there's no way to compete as an actor. What are you compe-ting against? In auto racing, either you win or you lose. You go across the finish line and come in first or second or ninth—or not at all." There is, however, the kind of satisfaction that comes from doing a role—from doing anything—well. "I suppose the final kick [is] to run a race or run one lap of a race and feel good about what you're able to do with that machinery. Somewhere along the line, I like to think that I went as fast as the car could go, that I went around there at the limit of my own adhesion. That gives me the same good feeling I have about myself that I have when I figure that I've licked a scene."

It was, he says, "four years after *Winning* that I found time to get a license and began to race," in 1972. He started at the bottom, driving a sedan in Sports Car Club of America races. In 1976 he won his first national amateur championship in the D Production Class. In 1977 he began to race with professionals. In 1979, at the age of fifty-four, he and his two codrivers finished second in the Le Mans 24-hour road race. They almost won when the leader's automobile was temporarily sidelined with fuel-injection problems. But then their similar 935 twin turbo Porsche developed engine troubles, and they were lucky to keep hold of second place as their automobile, which had reached speeds of up to 220 mph, virtually coasted across the finish line with a dying engine. He devoted 1984 to racing and in 1985 and 1986 won his third and fourth Sports Club of America national championships. He gave up regular racing on the circuit but is co-owner of the Newman-Hass Indy Car with drivers Mario and Michael Andretti, Nigel Mansell, and Paul Tracy. In February 1995, just after his seventieth birthday, he returned to driving and he and his Roush Racing team mates Mark Martin, Michael Brockman, and Tommy Kendall drove their Ford Cobra to victory in their class of automobile, and a third-overall finish, in the Rolex 24-hour endurance race in Daytona Beach, Florida, making Newman the oldest person ever to win a professionally sanctioned auto race.

His automobile was sponsored by Paramount Pictures, in grateful appreciation for the success of *Nobody's Fool*. After the Academy Award nominations were announced, a full-page ad in *The New York Times* headlined the two for the movie (Newman and director Robert Benton for best screenplay adaptation), then Newman's Best Actor awards from the New York Film Critics Circle and the National Society of Film Critics. In bold letters after that was, "Winner, GTS-1 24 Hours of Daytona." And in even bolder type, "Paul Newman." Only then did the ad get into the quotes of praise for the movie.

Winning (1969). The experience of doing the film led Newman to take up auto racing. Joanne Woodward has accepted his passion as a *fait accompli*, though she did once say, "A mind is a terrible thing to waste on a Trans Am motor."

Newman loves racing but hates the mobs of reporters and photographers that his presence draws, as much for what it does to other drivers as for what it does to him. His finishing so well at Le Mans, for instance, obscured the victory of the brothers Don and Bill Whittington. "My racing here places an unfortunate emphasis on the team," he said after the race, unsure if he would return again. "It takes away from the people who really do the work." He holds firmly to the notion that his racing is a special part of his life for himself, not the public, and his usual response to reporters trying to interview him at a track is, "Why do you want to talk to me? Because I'm a movie star?" As his accomplishments grew and he began to win titles, the question begged the notion that someone might want to ask him about his driving. But he is all too familiar with the public eye and desires to protect this interest as much as possible. Even on one of the very few occasions when a stranger's intrusion was amusing—Newman was rubbing ice cubes on his racing gloves to stiffen the leather and someone called out, "So that's why they call you Cool Hand Luke"—he didn't turn to see who made the comment, although he did gleefully repeat the line many times.

"I don't care what people say about my acting," he said at a race soon after Le Mans. "I've been humiliated, lied about; but when they mess around with my racing, that's something else."

Woodward's response to Newman's racing was to accept it as a *fait accompli* and make the best of it that she could, even though she did once say, "A mind is a terrible thing to waste on a Trans Am motor." For herself, she prefers the disguised power of ballet to the brute power of auto racing.

"She has just been the best of all things through this," Newman says. "But she's never put any kind of pressure on me to do anything other than what I'm doing. Well, I don't know if that's an accurate statement; yes, she *does* make requests. Now I enjoy all aspects of the theater, though after I'd seen *Giselle* for the nineteenth time, I became resistant. But Joanne and I have … [an] agreement. There are some things that I won't actually go to by myself, but I will with her." Such as? "The forty-sixth running of *Giselle*."

For most of the '70s and '80s Newman adapted his filming schedule so that he was free to race from May to October. If that meant that he made movies like *The Towering Inferno* (1974), *Quintet* (1979), and *When Time Ran Out* (1980), well, so be it. In fairness, during this time he also made *The Mackintosh Man* (1973), an espionage story directed by John Huston and written by Walter Hill; *The Sting* (1973) with Robert Redford; *Buffalo Bill and the Indians, Or Sitting Bull's History Lesson* (1976), written by Arthur Kupit and directed by Robert Altman; and was one of the many stars who made cameo appearances in Mel Brooks's *Silent Movie* (1976), in which the only word spoken is by the mime artist Marcel Marceau: "No." These make for a string of hits and misses not much different from any other decade in his career. What matters is that finding a passion for something other than the grind of movies seems to have had a beneficial effect not only on his racing, but on his acting as well. At least according to his wife, he says.

"Her theory is that I was getting bored as an actor, maybe because I couldn't get out of my skin any longer, and that I was starting to duplicate myself. She says that she thinks part of my passion for racing has now bled back into my acting."

There is good evidence to support that theory. One piece is that the early 1970s is when Newman began the shift from leading man to leading character. The weight of movies shifted from his handsome face and muscled shoulders to more subtle nuances of acting. This made room for very interesting performances, for it meant that without ever losing his authority as a star he could inhabit some original and quirky people.

Detective Dennis Murphy in *Fort Apache, the Bronx* (1981) is a good example. Murphy has spent fourteen of his eighteen years on the New York City Police force in the South Bronx precinct. It is the most blighted area of the city, decimated by highway construction in the 1950s, abandoned by the middle class in the 1960s, and reduced to smoke and rubble by arsonists in the 1970s. With whole blocks burned and leveled, it looks like Berlin at the end of World War II and is inhabited largely by impoverished blacks and Puerto Ricans. The frustration of the police and other social agencies in so hopeless a setting is evident. Murphy deals with all this as well as one can, in part by numbing himself with booze. When his young new partner tells him, "You have to get in touch with yourself," Murphy replies, "Every time I try, the line is busy."

But after years of staying uninvolved, Murphy suddenly finds himself torn in three directions. He falls in love with Isabella (Rachel Ticotin), a Puerto Rican nurse who secretly escapes the intense pressures of the hospital with an occasional injection of heroin, which leads to her death from a poisonous fix. He has an ongoing battle of wills with his commander, Connolly (Ed Asner). And, at the heart of things, he watches as two fellow cops throw a suspected felon off a roof and then has to decide whether to turn them in. Pauline Kael in *The New Yorker* called Newman's performance "near-great."

Steve McQueen was originally set to play Murphy, but after he dropped out Newman took the part for $3 million and a percentage of the gross profits. His reward besides the role and the money and wonderful reviews was his next movie. During the shooting of *Fort Apache* on location, irresponsible news accounts portrayed the movie as racist and brought about street protests, as well as a law suit by a citizens' committee against Newman and the production company.

"It's not a racist picture," he responded. "It is tough on Puerto Ricans, blacks, and the neighborhood, but the two villains are Irish cops who throw a Puerto Rican off a roof. Sure, there are Puerto Rican bankers in the South Bronx. But it's a cop movie and you can't have a Puerto Rican banker coming up to the desk sergeant and saying, 'I'm a Puerto Rican

RIGHT
In *The Mackintosh Man* (1973), an espionage thriller directed by John Huston. Newman has a reputation as a practical joker, and during filming he tossed a dummy dressed like himself from a seventy-foot-high balcony. After about fifteen seconds he "waved down at everybody gaily [but] it never occurred to me that someone—perhaps Huston—might have had a heart attack." It led him to tone down his pranks.

banker, and I'd like to give you a loan on your house in Hunt's Point.'" He also pointed out that there was neither a hospital nor a high school in the precinct and suggested that those wants might be more suitably addressed by the group.

The experience of dealing with a reckless newspaper led to the making of *Absence of Malice* (1981), in which Michael Gallagher, the son of a dead Mafioso, runs a legitimate business in Miami with his uncle, his only connection to the mob. But a federal investigator who thinks Gallagher knows something about the disappearance of a labor leader leaks not wholly truthful information to reporter Megan Carter (Sally Field) in the hope of pressuring Gallagher to cooperate. Megan publishes her story in the belief that her facts are correct, and after her mistake leads to the suicide of an innocent woman caught up in the chase Gallagher sets out to have his revenge on the investigator and on the newspaper.

Newman found that he now prepared for his roles differently. Instead of having to go on location early or get drunk on an airplane to fathom a character, after working so long as an actor "you don't have as much wasted effort. You don't play around as much. You kind of make a judgment as to what the core of the character is. Now, I don't know whether that's good or bad," he says with more modesty than is necessary, "it may also just be lazy." He says an example of judging a character's core is the way he has lawyer Frank Galvin follow a doctor down the street in *The Verdict*. Galvin desperately needs the doctor's testimony to save his case, and Newman says he played the scene "the way a dog follows somebody that has a bone in his hand—sideways." In *Absence of Malice*, he used his own physical traits for Michael Gallagher, only made them more economical. "He knew a lot," Newman explains, "and people who know a lot don't do very much with their bodies." He also feels his performances now are less self-conscious than earlier in his career, and he cites Galvin's dramatic summation before the jury, saying, "the emotions were there but you couldn't see the machinery."

For all the fist fights Newman has had in his life, what he has trouble with even now is being physically violent for the sake of a shot. It's one thing to hit a boxer in *Somebody Up There Likes Me* or pull a punch for *Harper*, but it's quite another actually to have to handle someone roughly. There is a point in *Absence of Malice* when Gallagher knocks down Megan and rips her blouse, which was very difficult for Newman to do convincingly. "He kept trying to fake it," Sally Field said afterward.

When he plays a historical character, such as the Louisiana governor Earl Long in *Blaze* or Leslie Groves, the Army general who oversaw the development of the atomic bomb at Los Alamos in *Fat Man and Little Boy*, he does his homework on the man. He reads about him, and, if possible, watches movie clips to get his speech patterns and the way he walks. "You find some essence of those guys and it percolates for a while," he says. Fictional characters, however, evolve out of his imagination.

Whether the character is real or fictional, the director Robert Benton says that "one of Paul's great strengths as an actor is that he has absolute compassion. It's reflected in his politics, it's reflected in his charitable activities. But as character does form us in whatever we pursue, it's that compassion for the people he plays that comes through. He doesn't play them from the outside. He inhabits them and believes in them. He doesn't try to find a defense for them." Some actors, Benton says, want their character to be sympathetic, even if he's a villain, as they "believe that no one *thinks* he is a villain. But Paul doesn't try to make him nicer than he is or more complex than he is; he just wants to understand the person he's playing, and by inhabiting and not judging him, bring a kind of compassion to him."

His Hank Stamper in *Sometimes a Great Notion* (1971) is an independent, difficult cuss with a social conscience the size of a flea's ear, a man willing to drive away his wife rather than abandon his principle, that principle being that the individual is greater than any other individual, not to mention the whole. He is an emotional focal point of the film but so, too, is Henry Fonda, who plays his equally stubborn father. These are men not of ideas but of rugged and physical labor that pits them against nature. Friendships and community are insignificant against something so great. Henry Stamper (Fonda) would rather die in a logging accident than be trimmed by society, and Hank is cut from the same cloth. These men are Ahabs of the forest.

Henry's arm is crushed by a tree and amputated. After his father's death and his wife's departure, Hank, regardless of the strike, takes a log-pack down the river. Henry's limb is tied to the mast of the tugboat, its raised middle finger an exclamation mark to his defiance. It is both a comical and a horrifying gesture, and it is just right.

Newman plays his part beautifully, something not normally remarkable, but he was by his own admission drinking far too much Scotch in this period. "For a while, it really screwed me up … hanging from chandeliers was not beyond the realm of possibility. A lot of bad stuff with cars. Generally boorish behavior," is about all he will say, adding, "I don't know why those times should be for public consumption." His greatest contribution to the movie, however, was made off the screen; he took over as director early in the shooting on location in Oregon because of differences with the original director, Richard Colla.

Newman says directing the movie, his second, "was a job I did not want or court. But what I was so afraid of was that some guy would come up there and then have us sit around on the clock for two weeks while he figured out what *he* wanted to do with the film." But directing was what he enrolled in at Yale, and what time has finally allowed him to do.

It was not an easy job. A week after taking over, Newman broke his ankle in a fall from a motorcycle while rehearsing a racing sequence. As he was to be in most of the remaining scenes, the production had to be shut down for several weeks until the plaster cast was removed. This was a blow to Newman, who prides himself on never missing a day and always being on time. He says that he missed only one performance (owing to flu) in four years on Broadway, and until the accident, only five days of shooting, all at once (flu again). Robert Benton, who directed him in *Nobody's Fool*, says, "Paul is the greatest gentleman I know. He's always on time, always gracious with everyone." Newman's example is the best authority any director has for keeping other stars prompt. When they're not, Newman will gently prod the habitually tardy himself; he once gave Robert Redford a framed needlepoint that reads, "Punctuality is the courtesy of kings."

Artistically, the antiauthoritarian, pro-individualist great notion of Ken Kesey's novel (he also wrote *One Flew Over the Cuckoo's Nest*) was hard to film faithfully. "I think I made a pretty good film," Newman says. "I don't know that it captured Kesey, but then the book was a kind of hallucination and there was simply no way I knew how to do that other than take a linear approach to it." In one memorable scene a felled tree knocks Hank's cousin (Richard Jaeckel) into shallow water and rolls onto his legs. Only Hank is around to help, but there is nothing he can do to move it. As the tide comes in, the vain hope is that the rising water will lift the log before the water covers his cousin's head.

Newman particularly likes the sequence. "One of the delights of that thing was when I went to the preview and it got to that scene. I looked down the row and people were pushing their feet under the seat in front of them. Everyone was trying to keep that log off him. It was *incredible* what they did to try to save that guy's life."

Comparing *Sometimes a Great Notion* to the genre of action movies in the 1930s about "tuna fishermen, bushpilots, high-wire repairmen, and just about any physical pursuit you can think of," Vincent Canby of *The New York Times* wrote that "Mr. Newman's handling of the logging and action sequences, some of which are as melodramatic as anything I've seen since Edward G. Robinson lost his hand in [Howard] Hawks's *Tiger Shark*, is also surprisingly effective, not because of any contemporary fanciness but because of what looks like straightforward confidence in the subject."

As Hank Stamper in *Sometimes a Great Notion* (1971), trying to keep the head of his cousin Joe Ben (Richard Jaeckel) above water in a rising tide after a tree Joe Ben felled rolled on to him. During the previews "I looked down the aisle and people were pushing their feet under the seat in front of them. Everyone was trying to get that log off him." It was the second film that Newman directed.

Hank Stamper was a sort of 1930s screen hero, but still within the Newman mold. But Reggie Dunlop in the thoroughly original *Slap Shot* (1977) wasn't. Dunlop is a thirty-nine-year-old washed-up player-coach of a very minor league hockey team, who favors tacky leather suits with bell-bottom trousers and whose vocabulary is built on a four-letter word. Reggie's locker-room mouth, which was completely appropriate to the character, was a shock to many Newman fans.

"Well, that has to be their problem," he says. "Hey. It was advertised as a locker-room picture and it *was* a locker-room picture and it was true to its origins. What I don't like is gratuitous language thrown into a film to make it rakish. When George Roy Hill gave me the script, he thought I would worry about the writing. And I said, 'Are you kidding? It's the most original thing I've read in I can't think how long. Of course I'll do it.'"

Newman relishes a story about trying to make the movie suitable for the severe time and language restrictions of network television. "There was a wonderful Hungarian editor named Andre who worked for ABC. And he called me and said, 'ABC has bought *Rachel, Rachel* for television. It's a wonderful movie, but I'm going to have to take twenty-three minutes out of it. Do you want to come down and help me, and you take it out rather than me?' I said, 'Yes, and thank you for the courtesy.'

"Twenty years later he called me again. 'Hi, this is Andre.' I said, 'Andre?' He said, 'Yes, ABC, we cut *Rachel* together.' I said, 'Oh, yeah, hi, how are you?' He said, 'We have just bought *Slap Shot*. It has 176 *fucks!*'"

Newman roars with laughter. "He didn't register a film by whether it had a good beginning, a middle, or end. But this film had 176 fucks and he just didn't know what to do with it. Ultimately George Hill got into it and we looped some of the words just to take some of the filth out of it. But what a wonderful movie it was. George does not think that it lost much in the television version. I thought it lost a lot."

The other two movies directed by Newman, *The Effect of Gamma Rays on Man-in-the-Moon Marigolds* (1972) and *Harry and Son* (1984), did not come together as well as *Rachel, Rachel* and *Sometimes a Great Notion*. The problem with *Marigolds*, really, is the material. Joanne Woodward plays Beatrice, a frumpy widow with two daughters whose antics are meant to shock and at the same time evoke pity. She is mean to others and herself, but she is also funny "in the manner of a quick-witted drag queen," as Canby put it, "which is one of the basic problems with frump plays as serious drama. How much of the time do we laugh at the frumps, and how much with them?... The basic material calls for a kind of second-rate bravura performance from everyone, from the production designer to the actors. There's no way to underplay it." Calling Newman a talented director "of plain, straight style," his kindest words were for Nell Potts, the Newmans' daughter Elinor, who played the sweeter of Beatrice's two girls with a "lovely, solemn performance in a film that otherwise successfully succeeds in being simultaneously barren and too busy, like Beatrice herself."

The biggest problem with *Harry and Son* is that it is weighed down by its earnestness. Newman is Harry and Woodward is his neighbor and friend of his wife, dead now two years. The conflict is between a son trying to find his way and a father who has one in mind for him. There is also a married daughter whom he has alienated. In some ways, the movie serves as the prequel to *Nobody's Fool*. Harry is a construction worker, the fellow who swings the wrecking ball from a crane. (There may be a metaphor in that.) He shares a house with his son, Howard (Robby Benson), who prefers surfing to an office job and works in a car wash so he can hit the beach more often. Howard's real goals are artistic, and at night he types away on a novel, an enterprise Harry doesn't understand. Each loves the other but can't find the words to say so.

"Valedictorian yesterday, car washer today," Harry tells Howard in disgust. "Get yourself a real job."

Harry, meanwhile, loses his job after an episode of recurring addled vision results in his nearly hitting a coworker with the wrecking ball, and he finds that now no one wants to hire him. He goes to see his brother Tom (Wilford Brimley), who runs a surplus business. Harry clearly doesn't like the surplus business.

"What do you do for kicks around here? Something's gotta give you a jolt. Shoplifters?"

Harry finally tells Tom that he's out of work because "my eyes went fuzzy on me again."

"Do you want to talk about it?" he asks.

"I just did."

Harry is not a great communicator, but then not many Newman characters are. Later he says, after Howard leaves a job, "Kids like you, nothing's too good for you. Kids like you are turning this country to Jell-O. It's a real hoot. I want to work and can't. You can work and don't."

Harry dies before he and his children are able to resolve their feelings. When the movie was released there was speculation that Newman, who cowrote the screenplay with Ronald L. Buck, drew on his relationship with his son, Scott, who died in 1978. Newman's response was direct: "You can't fictionalize grief," he said. If there is any parallel to Newman's life in *Harry and Son*, it is much more likely to be found in the relationship he had or didn't have with his father, not in what occurred with his son. The attitude toward surplus certainly mirrors Newman's feelings about his father's and uncle's company in Cleveland:

"Did you ever think about surplus?" Tom asks Howard.

"He thinks surplus ain't romantic," Harry interrupts (which happens to have been Newman's description years ago).

"Well, it's got its own kind of special allure, kid, let me tell you," his uncle says. But when Harry asks him to explain it, they all laugh.

The Color of Money (1986) with Tom Cruise was not a sequel to *The Hustler* but rather a pick-up on the life of Fast Eddie Felson twenty-five years later. After seven nominations, Newman finally won an Oscar for Best Actor.

Newman has always been guarded in discussing the details of his and Scott's estrangement. How does a young man find himself under a shadow so large? A father trying to help is often viewed by the son as a father trying to hinder. Scott was nineteen when Butch Cassidy, one of a generation of moviegoers' great romantic characters, held the land in thrall. By all accounts the two by that time had pretty much broken with each other. Scott was as handsome as Paul. He tried his hand at acting, worked as a stuntman, and under the name William Scott was a part-time nightclub singer.

Newman was at Kenyon College, directing a student play, when the call came telling him that Scott had died of an accidental overdose of drugs and alcohol.

When asked a few years after the event how he reacted to the moment, Newman replied tensely, "In a way, I had been waiting for the call for ten years. Somehow, my body mechanism built me an anesthetic for when it really happened. I was … a lot of things when I got that call. I was probably more pissed off than anything. … Scott and I had simply lost the ability to help each other. I had lost the ability to help him, and he had lost the ability to help himself. I had simply lost my ability to make a difference. Any kind of difference. … I just realized that whatever I was doing in trying to be helpful was not being helpful at all. In fact, it could have been harmful."

"We were like rubber bands," he said on another occasion, "one minute close, the next separated by an enormous and unaccountable distance. I don't think I'll ever escape the guilt."

Soon after Scott's death Newman donated or raised a total of $500,000 to set up the Scott Newman Foundation at the University of Southern California, which finances the production of anti-drug movies for children, and he continues to support it with some of the profits from the Newman's Own food line. His daughter Susan runs the Foundation. Newman stayed at Kenyon and directed the play before going on to the funeral. "There was nothing else I could do," he said. He had fought his own battle with alcohol off and on for years and now drinks only beer.

"It doesn't make any difference whether it's LSD or angel dust or cocaine or booze," he continued. "People are just looking around for a sledgehammer somewhere along the line. I gave up hard liquor. We were finishing shooting *Sometimes a Great Notion*. I don't know if it was the pressure of the picture but I was really out of line. I've always been fascinated with why one embraces the sledgehammer. ... They say you can take the kid out of Shaker Heights, but you can't take Shaker Heights out of the kid. Well, *oh yes, you can!* You can do that very simply with a good bottle of Scotch. Because then you can never tell what the kid's likely to do."

As a kid Newman seemed unlikely to become a bottle magnate, if only of salad dressings and sauces. It all started innocuously enough. His children liked his vinegar, oil, and herb dressing, so before he left home to make a movie he'd make up a big batch for them. Later he filled used wine bottles with his dressing and gave them to friends. It was a lark, even something of a joke, when he and A. E. Hotchner decided to package a few cases commercially and give whatever profits were made to charity. Within two months supermarkets all over America were clamoring for shipments of Newman's Own Olive Oil and Vinegar Dressing. Spaghetti sauce followed, then popcorn, lemonade, and salsa, and today there are nineteen products, with more on the way. Nell and Clea Newman are now involved with the company, too. The lark has become a legacy, the perfect ending for a man who loves jokes. There are twelve Newman's Own factories in North America and distribution to countries including Australia, Japan, Canada, China, France, Switzerland, Iceland, Great Britain, and Brazil.

"The fact that the food business produced this sudden windfall of profit jolted a slumbering desire in him to give back to the people who had given him such an extraordinary career," Hotchner says. "He became an accidental philanthropist."

Newman writes the fanciful label copy that borders on corny but is also quite amusing; for instance, this paean to Newman's Own Industrial Strength Venetian Spaghetti Sauce: "Working twelve-hour days ... wrecked ... hungry ... arrive home, deserted by wife and children ... cursing! Scan the cupboard—one package spaghetti ... one bottle marinara sauce ... run to the kitchen, cook—junk! YUK! Lie down, snooze ... visions of culinary delights ... Venetian ancestor tickles my ear, tickle, tickle ... sauce talk ... MAMA MIA! Dash to the vegetable patch ... yum yum ... boil water ... activate spaghetti ... ditto the sauce ... slurp, slurp ... Terrific! Magnifico! Slurp! Caramba! Bottle the sauce! ... share with guys on street car ... ah, me, finally immortal." For the popcorn he signs himself Col. "Pops" Newman. And for his new Caesar Salad Dressing he came up with a sketch of the dying Julius, a bloody dagger pointing at the ingredients, and a rewrite of the emperor's penultimate words: "Don't dilute us, Brutus."

As Newman's character Tony Lawrence says at the beginning of *The Young Philadelphians*, a man's life is the sum of his actions. In the case of an actor, it is easy to assume that the sum of his parts is his whole. That is a mistake with almost anyone, none more so than Newman. Generosity is not a hallmark of Newman's characters. Can you imagine Hud Bannon founding a camp for kids with leukemia and other catastrophic diseases of the blood? Fast Eddie making and bottling salad dressing to raise money for charities? Butch Cassidy being a financial angel for a political magazine? Cool Hand Luke campaigning for a nuclear freeze?

Newman's constant reference to luck is largely out of modesty but not without some merit when it comes to the good fortune of Newman's Own. What else besides luck can explain the phenomenal success of his products? Well, they're good, for one. For another, people like Newman, and they like the notion of buying something the profits of which go to help others; he feeds the haves, who in turn give him money to feed the have-nots. But appreciation aside, no one could have predicted that a movie star selling snacks and condiments made from his own recipes would engender a company that now gives away approximately $6 million annually, often to organizations outside the charitable mainstream in the

United States and abroad. Money is given for missionary vehicles in Ethiopia and buses for migrant workers in Florida, to kidney banks and hospitals, and for victims of natural disasters from Rwanda to San Francisco. There have been several hundred recipients over the years; recent ones include the Freestone Food Bank in Cincinnati, Ohio, Dignity House in Los Angeles, and the progeny of the Hole in the Wall Gang Camp. His focus of late has been on children's causes, the environment, the elderly, the homeless, and the establishment of other Hole in the Wall Gang Camps in Lake County, Florida, and County Kildare, Ireland. These camps could not be imagined by the most sentimental of writers; their spirit and heart-melting benefit to children who for the most part are gravely ill make Charles Dickens seem like a cynic.

The original Hole in the Wall Gang Camp in the village of Ashford in northeastern Connecticut was built after Newman received numerous requests for grants from parents of severely ill children. He was touched by their plight, but American tax law does not permit Newman's Own and similar groups to make contributions to individuals.

In 1987, finding the food company more profitable than they had ever imagined, Newman and Hotchner decided that in addition to supporting other charities they wanted one of their own, and thus the idea of a camp for kids too sick to attend a conventional one was born. Their decisions are made not in some vast corporate structure but in a tiny office originally furnished with a Ping-Pong table and chairs from Newman's pool, near their homes in Westport, Connecticut. The office is a little bigger now, but the furniture is still there and Newman's desk continues to have an umbrella over it. These days, around 2,400 applications for grants arrive every year. In the middle of December Newman and Hotchner sit down and decide where the money will go. Newman refuses to have a staff to sort through them because, he says, "It would take all the fun out of it." It would also deny him the pleasure of deciding that a struggling organization is worth supporting even though it has not applied for help. Carroll Brewster, the executive director of the Hole in the Wall Gang Fund, tells how Newman delights in spontaneously writing, say, a $25,000 check for a small community health clinic he has just been told about. In the case of the clinic, the money arrived out of the blue just before Christmas, a touch Newman enjoyed.

"I don't think of myself as charitable," Newman says, "I think of myself as whimsical, and

BELOW AND
RIGHT
**The brightly painted and
immaculately kept Hole
in the Wall Gang Camp
in Connecticut, for children
too ill to attend a
conventional camp, looks
like a turn-of-the-century
Oregon lumber town.
Only on second or third
glance does one notice
that the trails are wide
enough for wheelchairs,
that walkways end in
access ramps, and the
washrooms in all thirty-
five buildings have
emergency buttons. The
theater is designed so
that one can go from the
front to the stage without
climbing a step. The
infirmary can handle the
specific requirements of
each of the 125 campers.
"It's OK to go there,"
an early camper said,
which is why it's called
the OK Corral.**

I wish that this charitable impulse could be tracked down to some spiritual fulfillment or some kind of Florence Nightingale syndrome. But it isn't. You just wake up one morning and it's there and you simply act on it. I've always felt guilty that there wasn't a stronger impulse underneath it." When it is suggested that, considering what has been accomplished, perhaps there doesn't need to be one, he responds, "Well, that's the way I feel. The camp was the same way. I just woke up one morning and said, 'We really ought to build one of these things.'" It is not surprising that the closest explanation he can articulate for creating the camp is "to acknowledge luck: the chance of it, the benevolence of it in my life, and the brutality of it in the lives of others; made especially savage for children because they may not be allowed the good fortune of a lifetime to correct it."

In the same way that things magically fall together when Mickey Rooney and Judy Garland decide to put on a show in an Andy Hardy movie, the Hole in the Wall Gang Camp went from an idea in 1987 to what looks like a turn-of-the-century Oregon lumber town of thirty-five buildings, in June 1988. Its creation shows what star power focused on an unselfish end can accomplish. Newman's Own put up $8 million of the $17 million it cost to build and endow the 300-acre camp, and help came from all over. Every school system in Connecticut raised money in amounts from $20 to $15,000. Barbers held "cut-a-thons;" school kids washed automobiles. Anheuser-Busch, the makers of Budweiser beer (which

Newman drinks) gave the money for the red octagonal dining hall with a 60-foot ceiling and a fireplace in a corner with sofas. Fatigue is sudden for these kids, and it offers them a place to lie down and not miss the camaraderie of meals. The Konover Construction Corporation, which built the camp, donated $1 million in material and services. A consortium of swimming-pool contractors donated the $250,000 Olympic-sized pool. Thirty-five Seabees from the Naval Submarine Base in Groton, Connecticut, volunteered their help to clear trails and build a footbridge and a floating dock. And Khaled Alhegelan, a twenty-six-year-old Saudi Arabian living in America, who has a rare blood disease that limited his childhood outdoor activities to a daily trip to a golf course with a fifty-year-old companion, was so taken with the idea that children with diseases like his could have fun together and not have to grow up alone that he appealed to the Saudi royal family for help. Two weeks later they sent a check for $5 million.

The camp was designed by Thomas Beeby, the dean of the Yale University School of Architecture. Painted in bright colors and immaculately kept up, it looks either like the lumber town it's meant to be or a perfect movie set. Or both. It is so beautifully done that it takes a second or third glance to realize that the trails are wide and smooth enough for wheelchairs and golf carts, that walkways end in access ramps, and that the washrooms have emergency buttons. Fifteen log-cabin bunkhouses, which sleep eight campers and four

counselors each, circle an open playing field that neither obtrusively nor coincidentally can serve as a landing area for a helicopter in an emergency. Campers, who range in age from seven to seventeen, are grouped by gender, age and, most importantly, so that not too many desperately sick kids are in any one cabin. Four buildings that look like frontier storefronts stepped down a small hill are really one big arts and crafts area inside, with ramps so that those in wheelchairs can easily get from one level to another. There is a forty-seven-acre pond for fishing. The horse ring is covered to shelter radiation and chemotherapy patients from the rain and sun. The swimming pool is specially heated and treated so that children with sickle-cell anemia are able to swim, sometimes for the first time in their lives, and so that there is no chemical effect on campers with external catheters. You can go from the front of the theater to the stage without climbing a step. And the infirmary, designed as a nineteenth-century lumber mill, can handle the specific medical requirements of each of the 125 campers, many of whom may require up to twenty medications a day. Chemotherapy is also administered, but there is no antiseptic smell or hospital look to the building. "It's OK to go there," an early camper said, which is why it is named the OK Corral.

The medical director is Dr. Howard Pearson, the head of Yale-New Haven Hospital's pediatrics department, professor of pediatrics at the Yale University School of Medicine, and a leading authority on children's cancer and diseases of the blood. Pearson carves a totem pole every summer, commemorating significant events in the life of the camp. The fifteen bunkhouses are divided into five groups—purple, red, blue, green, and yellow—and loyalties to each become fierce, with banners in the dining hall and gym proclaiming their excellence. One tacked up in the gym in the summer of 1994 read, "Purple, it's not just for bruises anymore." For children whose diseases usually make them pariahs at school, the camp is a life-changing experience.

"Positive trauma," is Brewster's term for this antidote to the emotional effects of the intrusive procedures that cancer patients suffer. Brewster tells of a letter he received from one camper's father: "I didn't recognize the child you sent home to me. Before he went to camp he needed walkers and had a feeding tube in his nose. One evening, the tube was knocked out during some boisterous play in the cabin. The doctor said it could wait until the morning to be replaced. By the time it was supposed to be done, he was in the mess hall eating a peach. Then he lost one walker and didn't bother to replace it. He was terribly shy before he went to camp. He wouldn't answer the phone, and he'd go to another room when the doorbell rang. Now he answers both."

"This is a place where 'How are you?' is not a casual question," Brewster says. "I thought at first it would just be a place for fun, but it's much more than that. Kids get a completely new sense of their identity in twelve days. They arrive here a victim and go home a hero." Everyone gets an award for something, from real musical ability to simply "great hugs." Campers pay no money to attend the eleven-night, twelve-day sessions but are asked to pay for transportation. Those unable to do so are helped. Immunology sessions (AIDS is never mentioned to avoid a sense of discrimination) last a week. These campers are mostly minorities from inner cities, and almost all are orphans.

The six camp sessions run from 1 June to 1 September. During the off-seasons there are medical conferences, special programs for parents, and a camp twice a year for three weeks for fifty or sixty inner-city children from Hartford that is like an alternative school. After one such camp, Newman recalls, "I put a little kid on the bus. I said, 'What's the best thing that happened to you?' And he said, 'I haven't heard a gunshot for three weeks.' So when you talk about kids with life-threatening diseases, a city itself may be a life-threatening disease."

During the summer Newman makes a point of attending virtually every session and stays the night. "It's a Paul Newman that no one would recognize," says A. E. Hotchner. "When he gets there, there is a transition to almost being a kid again himself. The children react to that and he gets down to their level. If they're painting their faces, he paints his face. If they're sitting around the fire telling stories, he does that. He's built his own place there where he can stay and I think it's a rejuvenation for him. It's not a sad place. The kids are having a good time. And I think that Paul gets more satisfaction out of a day there than he would out of winning the Academy Award." Newman's greatest contribution, though, may be the support he gives the people who work there. "He's a gentle, inspiring, elder statesman who interacts with the potentially harried staff," Brewster says. "If a counselor has been up three nights in a row sitting with a kid, he finds that person to say what a great job he or she is doing. He has been there since the start, and when he says, 'I understand how difficult it is,' that rings true. He's endlessly empowering and inspiring."

Newman likes to spend time in the mess hall, where girls and boys sit at picnic tables under the cupola atop the barnlike building. On a wall is an antlered felt moose head with a sign hanging around its neck put there by some campers: "Newmoose," it says. On its head is always one of the hats Newman brings to camp; a fireman's hat on a recent visit. The campers are often some of the few people on earth who don't know who Paul Newman is. When he was first told this by a staff member some years ago, Newman's jaw dropped. A moment later he smiled and said, "Of course they don't!"

One day Newman sat at lunch and struck up a conversation with a bald-headed boy from the inner city. Cartons of Newman's Own Old Fashioned Roadside Virgin Lemonade, made, the label says, according to an old Woodward family recipe, are as ubiquitous in the camp as trees and maybe more so than water. As the boy refilled his glass with lemonade he noticed the sketch of Newman's face on a panel of the container, the spot where, on millions of milk cartons in the USA, a picture of a missing child appears. He looked at Newman, looked back at the sketch, and then asked, very worried, "Oh, Paul, are you lost?"

Newman likens the turn his charitable work has taken to the way a character in the mind of a writer suddenly takes on a life of its own and tells the writer what it is doing, rather than the reverse.

"I've just started to write a little bit, a screenplay," he says. "I'm conversant with the way a character surprises you sometimes when you act. But I'm equally surprised by characters and situations that suddenly develop a mind of their own and carry you into places that you just don't expect. And that's really what happened to the camp. Like a character saying, 'No,

I'm sorry, I'm going over here.' So you say, 'Well, if you want to go over there, what the hell, go over there. See what it's like.'" He suggests that may be the reason why the pattern of support from Newman's Own "seems directionless sometimes, or splattered." In fact, it just seems reactive to whatever needs to be done.

There is a sense in *Nobody's Fool* that some resolution has come to Newman. Robert Benton, who has known Newman for more than twenty years, says, "It's about a man who has come to terms with his own life, and Paul, who says he has been extraordinarily fortunate, has also had an enormous struggle. What that struggle is, I don't know. I'm very careful with all actors to know only as much as is good for me. But I do believe that Paul figured it out and used his life."

The character of Sully is the cinematic father to a saloon full of younger Newman roles. He is stubborn, selfish, willful and, in the way only Newman can play these men, completely charming in spite of himself. Sully is a part-time construction worker with a bum knee who, not entirely without reason, many years ago walked out on his wife and son and has come to live with Miss Beryl (Jessica Tandy), his eighth-grade teacher, who continues to believe in him even though everyone else has their doubts, Sully included. He has a love-hate relationship with Carl (Bruce Willis), the owner of the Tip Top Construction Company, and a competition that expresses itself in their alternately stealing a snow blower from each other. Carl fools around on the side, and his wife (Melanie Griffith) and Sully have a sweet but unfulfilled romance themselves. One day during rehearsal, Benton had Newman and Ms. Griffith exchange roles. Despite her sexuality and looks, Benton felt she was really one of the guys. "It turned out they were interchangeable," Benton says. "She was like Jean Arthur in *Only Angels Have Wings*."

Sully's son, Peter (Dylan Walsh), and his wife and two boys appear in the small upstate New York town to celebrate Thanksgiving with his mother, and Peter and his son Will (Alexander Goodwin) are the kindling that fires the story. Through his shy and fearful grandson, Sully finds a way home to his own son. The entire plot of *Nobody's Fool* is really about the arc of Sully's evolution into a man who acknowledges the importance of the lives of others in his own, and who late in life realizes that love can actually be received and given. Except for two scenes, Newman is in every moment of the picture, and therefore he was required to modulate his progression carefully. Yet the movie was shot in a very piece-meal way. The other stars, some of whom were working for nearly the minimum wage, had to be scheduled according to their availability, and all their scenes were done at once. Although it does not show in the movie, Miss Tandy was very ill at the time, and she died before the picture was released.

"From an actor's point of view, the picture was done under terrible circumstances," Benton says. "It had to be shot in blocks having to do with actors who were coming in to work. We had to do the beginning and the end in the first two weeks, and we never got to the story with the son until we were three-quarters done. In the old days in Hollywood, when players were under contract, you'd just work your way through the picture and there was a sense of growing progression day by day. Here it all had to be thought out. It was like playing chess by mail."

What made it possible were the hours and hours that Newman and Benton both spent discussing Sully. Benton, who grew up in rural Texas and is more than passingly familiar with reticent blue-collar types, also wrote the screenplay from Richard Russo's novel. "Having written the script," he says, "the first thing I did was just listen to Paul talk about Sully, about what guys like this

As Donald "Sully" Sullivan in *Nobody's Fool* (1994), about a man who has been emotionally inaccessible to his son and finds through his timid grandson a way to remedy that. Director Robert Benton thought Newman drew heavily on himself to play Sully. "Well," Newman says, "let's just say that the progression of this character goes from not being available to becoming available, and that's too close for comfort."

were like. He'd use analogies of guys on the race circuit and his friends in various places. Then I would use examples of people I have known. And we would talk back and forth, and each one of these things that worked was a building block. Early on, I did a big aria where Sully explains himself, and Paul said, 'We cannot write a character who is more articulate than that character would be in real life. He is a man who shouldn't be able to explain him-self. We have to find other ways to explain him.' Which was absolutely dead-on right. It put an extraordinary restriction on me, but it made the character better and truer. In the world I grew up in, people were not that articulate. They were not able to explain themselves that well."

The task, then, was for Newman to find a way to explain Sully not through words but through nuance. Benton adds, "Robert Altman once said that the only real heroes in movies are the actors. It's easy for us to make up dialogue and shoot it, but the actors are the ones who have to get in front of the camera and make an audience believe that it's real. There came a point where all the talking back and forth was really me being a sounding board for him. I simply was an editor for him at that point. I would say what didn't work for me, but generally he did nine-tenths of the work. He pokes around and pokes around and pokes around, looking for things from his past, or things from his friends."

One of Benton's greatest desires was for Newman to make Sully a protagonist like Lew Harper or Frank Galvin, not a finely wrought character like Leslie Groves or Earl Long. "I wanted that Paul back again. I wanted Paul within the tradition of Paul. For Sully, what I really wanted Paul to draw on was Fast Eddie and Cool Hand Luke and Harper and that group, that outside quality that he has sympathy with. The character he plays is forever outside, forever ambitious, forever wanting something he cannot have, even if it's order, or to be listened to."

Newman was willing to do whatever it took to get that. Sully is sixty years old. Newman, who looks barely that, had his sixty-ninth birthday while making the film, and Woodward and their children came to the location in Beacon, New York, to go to dinner with him. But Newman was rehearsing the next day's work, Benton says, "and we got stuck on something and we couldn't get out of it, and he simply stayed there and blew off his own birthday."

"Sully was a lot of luck," Newman says, ever consistent. "Everything was shot out of continuity. Even though you have the benefit of some rehearsal, still scenes were rewritten and scenes that you had rehearsed were lifted out and scenes that hadn't been written were put in. Then the whole ending was reshot. It validates the theory that chaos is a very orderly process. That probably describes that movie," he chuckles. "I'm not saying there was anything defective. It's just that there was a mountain of material. The piece was basically thrustless.

"If you go into a picture and at the beginning of the picture you don't have the money and during the picture you find ways to get the money and at the end of the picture you've got the money, you'd have a very active line that you could pursue. There are so many things you can do: you can seduce, you can threaten, you can maul, you can be devious, you can be crafty: you've got active things to do. But try to figure out, how do you play going from being inaccessible to accessible," he laughs. "That's finally the thrust of the film, isn't it? And, if something is lifted out that you've rehearsed at the beginning of the thing and replaced with something else ..." he trails off and shrugs. "That's why I say, I think there was a lot of instinct, and maybe that's what forty years of films does: that you're really running on just pure gall and something intuitive. I don't know what it is."

Newman's conflict encompasses both his life and his work. Frequently in the past fifteen years or so he has given thoughts to leaving acting and finding something completely different to do. Aquafarming, of all things, is one thing he's mentioned, but never underestimate Newman's sense of whimsy.

In the end, though, he has stayed on, delivering even richer performances as the years pass. He says that if he identifies with anyone, it is not another actor or a character he has played but Tonio Kröger, the protagonist of the eponymous Thomas Mann story written at the turn of the century.

Tonio writes in a letter to his friend Lisaveta Ivanova, who once called him a failed bourgeois: "I stand between two worlds. I am at home in neither, and this makes things a little difficult for me. You artists call me a bourgeois, and the bourgeois feel they ought to arrest me. ... I don't know which of the two hurts more bitterly. The bourgeois are fools; but you worshippers of beauty, you who say I am phlegmatic and have no longing in my soul, you should remember that there is a kind of artist so profoundly, so primordially fated to be an artist that no longing seems sweeter and more precious to him than his longing for the bliss of the commonplace."

"The bourgeois think we're revolutionaries," Newman says more simply, "and the bohemians see that we have a lot of Jell-O and don't wear neckerchiefs and they think we're bourgeois."

Of his work and life, Newman says, "Sometimes I feel it's all here, the next day that it's garbage. One minute you take all this stuff you've been through—all the experience, some of the pain, some of the laughter—and you put it all out on the floor for everyone to look at; the next minute, you say it's just a game. Even in a really emotional scene there is fifteen to twenty percent of you standing back like a camera. One side of you is always looking at the other and going, 'tsk, tsk, tsk.' It's a very funny existence—you can't feel very stable about yourself."

But it is also an existence that, despite any instability, he's lived well for forty years now. Anyway, a career change so late in life is difficult to pull off, especially when you do what you have been doing better than ever. For all the talk of aquafarming and other non-show-business endeavors, Newman at heart seems to know that he is committed to his own craft.

"There's an old joke about a traveling salesman," he said some fifteen years ago when he was pondering a change, but it is all the more apt today because he still hasn't made one. "He comes home and finds his wife in a state of déshabillé and the bed slightly rumpled. He throws open a closet door and sees this guy standing there, his knees shaking. 'What are you doing here?' he demands. And the guy says, 'A fella's gotta be someplace.' So why am I still acting? Well, like he said, a fella's gotta be someplace."

He is seventy now and wears his age gracefully and graciously, although he does say, "I can't think of anything that gets better with ageing. I'm not mellower, I'm not less angry, I'm not less self-critical, I'm not less tenacious." His hair is more white than grey, and it has thinned, something he does nothing to hide either in his movies or in life.

He long ago gave up the VW with the Porsche engine. Now he drives a Volvo station wagon that looks the perfect model of suburban transportation, at least until you listen to the motor and realize that the engine is packed with racing power. Mention to him that it sounds like that and he gives a smile of elegant satisfaction and boyish joy. This actually is something of a metaphor for Newman, whose outward looks conceal his inward drive.

Newman sat one day in the barn at his Connecticut home, surrounded by captured moments of his life. One wall holds the photographs and awards of his racing, as if that is a private sidelight. A larger wall is covered with snapshots of family and friends and colleagues on various movies, but nothing is so full as his life. Even so, there appear to be significant spots where complete fulfillment will always be denied.

Fathers and sons are the focal points of so many Newman films. None is more emotionally affecting than *Nobody's Fool* because none rings truer to life. But movies by necessity settle relationships, and however much Sully and Newman may have in common, Newman will never have the grace of resolution with his own father that Sully's son has with him. It is something he gives thought to, and while that relationship is hardly the force that drives Newman, it makes for an interesting place to stand for a perspective on him. The journey from Shaker Heights has had all the romance and newness that retailing lacked, and still more is promised. What would Arthur Newman have thought of all that has become of his troubled younger son? Newman has an idea.

"It's always been one of the great losses in my life that my father … you know, he died when he was fifty-seven … was not around to see what has happened," he said slowly. "I think he would have been one of the few people in the family who would have really appreciated how complicated the process has been in this trajectory. He would have admired and recognized the luck, the tenaciousness, the good fortune, the appearance. But he would have understood all those factors and would have been able to delight in it, I think."

At the Cannes Film Festival in 1987, during which the Newman-directed *The Glass Menagerie* was shown. Newman has starred in one Broadway production and two film adaptations of Tennessee Williams' work. He made the film to preserve Joanne Woodward's stage performance.

Plays & Films

■ PICNIC
by William Inge
Staged by Joshua Logan; scenery and lighting by Jo Mielziner; costumes by Mildred Trebor; presented by the Theater Guild and Mr. Logan. Opened 19 February 1953 at the Music Box.

■ THE DESPERATE HOURS
by Joseph Hayes, based on his novel
Staged by Robert Montgomery; setting and lighting by Howard Bay; costumes by Robert Randolph; produced by Howard Erskine and Mr. Hayes. Opened 10 February 1955 at the Ethel Barrymore Theater.

■ SWEET BIRD OF YOUTH
by Tennessee Williams, with music by Paul Bowles
Staged by Elia Kazan; scenery and lighting by Jo Mielziner; presented by Cheryl Crawford; costumes by Anna Hill Johnstone. Opened 10 March 1959 at the Martin Beck Theater.

■ BABY WANT A KISS
by James Costigan
Staged by Frank Corsaro; presented by the Actors Studio Inc.; scenery and costumes by Peter Harvey; lighting by David Hays. Opened 19 April 1964 at the Little Theater.

■ THE SILVER CHALICE
(1954) Color, 144 minutes, Warner Bros.
Directed by Victor Saville; screenplay by Lesser Samuels, from the novel by Thomas B. Costain; produced by Victor Saville.

■ THE RACK
(1956) B&W, 100 minutes, Metro-Goldwyn-Mayer
Directed by Arnold Lavan; screenplay by Stewart Stern; based on the television play by Rod Serling; produced by Arthur M. Loew.

■ SOMEBODY UP THERE LIKES ME
(1956) B&W, 113 minutes, Metro-Goldwyn-Mayer
Directed by Robert Wise; screenplay by Ernest Lehman; based on the autobiography of Rocky Graziano, written with Rowland Barber; produced by Charles Schnee.

■ THE HELEN MORGAN STORY
(1957) B&W, 118 minutes, Warner Bros.
Directed by Michael Curtiz; screenplay by Oscar Saul, Dean Riesner, Stephen Longstreet and Nelson Gidding; produced by Martin Rackin.

■ UNTIL THEY SAIL
(1957) B&W, 96 minutes, Metro-Goldwyn-Mayer
Directed by Robert Wise; screenplay by Robert Anderson, based on the story by James A. Michener; produced by Charles Schnee.

- **CAT ON A HOT TIN ROOF**
(1958) Color, 108 minutes,
Metro-Goldwyn-Mayer
*Directed by Richard Brooks;
screenplay by Richard Brooks
and James Poe; based on the
play by Tennessee Williams;
cinematography by William
Daniels; edited by Ferris Webster;
produced by Lawrence
Weingarten.*

- **THE LEFT-HANDED GUN**
(1958) B&W, 102 minutes,
Warner Bros.
*Directed by Arthur Penn;
screenplay by Leslie Stevens,
based on the teleplay* **The Death
of Billy the Kid** *by Gore Vidal;
cinematography by Peverell
Marley; edited by Folmar
Blangsted;
produced by
Fred Coe.*

- **THE LONG, HOT SUMMER**
(1958) Color, 117 minutes,
Twentieth Century-Fox
*Directed by Martin Ritt;
screenplay by Irving Ravetch
and Harriet Frank Jr., based
on* **Barn Burning**, **The Spotted
Horse** *and* **The Hamlet** *by
William Faulkner;
cinematography by Joseph
LaShelle; edited by Louis
Loeffler; produced by Jerry Wald.*

- **RALLY ROUND THE
FLAG, BOYS!**
(1958) Color, 106 minutes,
Twentieth Century-Fox
*Directed and produced by Leo
McCarey; screenplay by Claude
Binyon and Leo McCarey, from
the novel by Max Shulman.*

- **THE YOUNG
PHILADELPHIANS**
(1959) B&W, 136 minutes,
Warner Bros.
*Directed by Vincent Sherman;
screenplay by James Gunn, from
the novel* **The Philadelphian** *by
Richard Powell.*

- **EXODUS**
(1960) Color, 212 minutes,
United Artists
*Directed and produced by Otto
Preminger; screenplay by Dalton
Trumbo, based on the novel by
Leon Uris; cinematography by
Sam Leavitt; edited by
Louis Loeffler; music by
Ernest Gold.*

- **FROM THE TERRACE**
(1960) Color, 144 minutes,
Twentieth Century-Fox
*Directed and produced by
Mark Robson; screenplay by
Ernest Lehman, from the
novel by John O'Hara.*

- **THE HUSTLER**
(1961) B&W, 133 minutes,
Twentieth Century-Fox
*Directed and produced by Robert
Rossen; screenplay by Robert
Rossen and Sidney Carroll, based
on the novel by Walter Tevis;
cinematography by Eugene
Schuftan; edited by Dede Allen.*

- **PARIS BLUES**
(1961) B&W, 98 minutes,
United Artists
*Directed by Martin Ritt;
screenplay by Jack Sher, Irene
Kamp, and Walter Bernstein,
adapted by Lulla Rosenfeld
from a novel by Harold Flender;
produced by Sam Shaw, George
Glass, and Walter Seltzer.*

- **HEMINGWAY'S
ADVENTURES OF A YOUNG
MAN,** also known as
**ADVENTURES OF A YOUNG
MAN**
(1962) Color, 140 minutes,
Twentieth Century-Fox
*Directed by Martin Ritt;
screenplay by A. E. Hotchner,
based on stories by Ernest
Hemingway; produced by
Jerry Wald.*

- **SWEET BIRD OF YOUTH**
(1962) Color, 120 minutes,
Metro-Goldwyn-Mayer
*Directed by Richard Brooks;
screenplay by Richard Brooks,
based on the stage play by
Tennessee Williams;
cinematography by Milton
Krasner; edited by Henry Berma;
produced by Pandro S. Berman.*

LEFT

**As Tony Lawrence in *The
Young Philadelphians* (1959).**

■ **HUD**
(1963) B&W, 112 minutes,
Paramount Pictures
*Directed by Martin Ritt;
screenplay by Irving Ravetch and
Harriet Frank Jr., adapted from
the novel* **Horseman, Pass By** *by
Larry McMurtry; cinematography
by James Wong Howe; edited by
Frank Bracht; music by Elmer
Bernstein; produced by Martin
Ritt and Irving Ravetch.*

■ **A NEW KIND OF LOVE**
(1963) Color, 110 minutes,
Paramount Pictures
*Directed and produced by
Melville Shavelson; screenplay
by Melville Shavelson.*

■ **THE PRIZE**
(1963) Color, 136 minutes,
Metro-Goldwyn-Mayer
*Directed by Mark Robson;
screenplay by Ernest Lehman,
based on the novel by Irving
Wallace; produced by Pandro
S. Berman.*

■ **THE OUTRAGE**
(1964) B&W, 97 minutes,
Metro-Goldwyn-Mayer
*Directed by Martin Ritt;
screenplay by Michael Kanin,
based on the film* **Rashomon,**
*directed by Akira Kurosawa, and
the play* **Rashomon,** *by Fay and
Michael Kanin; produced by A.
Ronald Lubin.*

■ **WHAT A WAY TO GO!**
(1964) Color, 111 minutes,
Twentieth Century-Fox
*Directed by J. Lee Thompson;
screenplay by Betty Comden and
Adolph Green, based on a story
by Gwen Davis; cinematography
by Leon Shamroy; edited by
Marjorie Fowler; music by
Nelson Riddle; produced by
Arthur P. Jacobs.*

■ **LADY L**
(1965) Color, 107 minutes,
Metro-Goldwyn-Mayer
*Directed by Peter Ustinov;
screenplay by Peter Ustinov,
based on the novel by
Romain Gary; produced by
Carlo Ponti.*

■ **HARPER**
(1966) Color, 121 minutes,
Warner Bros.
*Directed by Jack Smight;
screenplay by William Goldman,
based on the novel* **The Moving
Target** *by Ross MacDonald;
cinematography by Conrad Hall;
edited by Stefan Arnsten; music
by Johnny Mandel; produced by
Elliott Kastner and Jerry
Gershwin.*

■ **TORN CURTAIN**
(1966) Color, 128 minutes,
Universal Pictures
*Directed and produced by Alfred
Hitchcock; screenplay by Brian
Moore.*

■ **COOL HAND LUKE**
(1967) Color, 126 minutes,
Warner Bros.-Seven Arts
*Directed by Stuart Rosenberg;
screenplay by Donn Pearce
and Frank S. Pierson, based
on the novel by Donn Pearce;
cinematography by Conrad Hall;
edited by Sam O'Steen; music by
Lalo Schifrin; produced by
Gordon Carroll.*

■ **HOMBRE**
(1967) Color, 111 minutes,
Twentieth Century-Fox
*Directed by Martin Ritt;
screenplay by Irving Ravetch
and Harriet Frank Jr., from
the novel by Elmore Leonard;
produced by Martin Ritt and
Irving Ravetch.*

■ **RACHEL, RACHEL**
(1968) Color, 101 minutes,
Kayos/Seven Arts
*Directed and produced by Paul
Newman; screenplay by Stewart
Stern, based on the novel* **A Jest
of God** *by Margaret Laurence;
cinematography by Gayne
Rescher; edited by Dede Allen;
music by Jerome Moross, Erik
Satie and Robert Schumann; art
direction by Robert Gundlach;
costumes by Domingo Rodriguez.*

■ **THE SECRET WAR OF
HARRY FRIGG**
(1968) Color, 110 minutes,
Universal Pictures
*Directed by Jack Smight;
screenplay by Peter Stone and
Frank Tarloff, from a story by
Frank Tarloff; produced by Hal
E. Chester.*

■ **BUTCH CASSIDY AND THE
SUNDANCE KID**
(1969) Color, 110 minutes,
Twentieth Century-Fox
*Directed by George Roy Hill;
screenplay by William Goldman;
cinematography by Conrad Hall;
edited by Richard C. Meyer;
music by Burt Bacharach;
produced by John Foreman, Paul
Newman co-executive producer.*

■ **WINNING**
(1969) Color, 123 minutes,
Newman-Foreman/Universal
Pictures
*Directed by James Goldstone;
screenplay by Howard Rodman;
produced by John Foreman, Paul
Newman co-executive producer.*

■ **KING: A FILMED RECORD
... MONTGOMERY TO
MEMPHIS**
(1970) A documentary on the life
of Dr. Martin Luther King
Narrated by Paul Newman.

■ **WUSA**

(1970) Color, 115 Minutes, Paramount Pictures

Directed by Stuart Rosenberg; screenplay by Robert Stone, from his novel **A Hall of Mirrors**; *cinematography by Richard Moore; music by Lalo Schifrin; produced by Paul Newman and John Foreman.*

■ **SOMETIMES A GREAT NOTION**

(1971) Color, 115 minutes, Universal Pictures

Directed by Paul Newman; screenplay by John Gay, based on the novel by Ken Kesey; cinematography by Richard Moore; edited by Bob Wyman; music by Henry Mancini; produced by John Foreman, Paul Newman co-executive producer.

■ **THEY MIGHT BE GIANTS**

(1971) Color, 88 minutes, Universal Pictures

Directed by Anthony Harvey; screenplay by James Goldman, based on his play; cinematography by Victor J. Kemper; edited by Gerald Greenberg; music by John Barry; produced by John Foreman (Paul Newman coproducer).

■ **THE EFFECT OF GAMMA RAYS ON MAN-IN-THE-MOON MARIGOLDS**

(1972) Color, 101 minutes, Newman-Foreman/Twentieth Century-Fox

Directed and produced by Paul Newman, John Foreman executive producer; screenplay by Alvin Sargent, based on the play by Paul Zindel; cinematography by Adam Holender; edited by Evan Lottman; music by Maurice Jarre.

■ **THE LIFE AND TIMES OF JUDGE ROY BEAN**

(1972) Color, 120 minutes, a First Artists Production, distributed by National General Pictures

Directed by John Huston; screenplay by John Milius; cinematography by Richard Moore; edited by Hugh S. Fowler; music by Maurice Jarre; produced by John Foreman, Paul Newman co-executive producer.

■ **POCKET MONEY**

(1972) Color, 102 minutes, a First Artists Production, distributed by National General Pictures

Directed by Stuart Rosenberg; screenplay by Terry Malick, based on the novel **Jim Kane** *by J. P. S. Brown, adapted by John Gay; cinematography by Laszlo Kovacs; edited by Robert Wyman; produced by John Foreman, Paul Newman co-executive producer.*

■ **THE MACKINTOSH MAN**

(1973) Color, 100 minutes, Warner Bros.

Directed by John Huston; screenplay by Walter Hill, based on the novel **The Freedom Trap** *by Desmond Bagley; cinematography by Oswald Morris; edited by Russell Lloyd; music by Maurice Jarre; produced by John Foreman.*

■ **THE STING**

(1973) Color, 129 minutes, a Richard D. Zanuck–David Brown presentation, distributed by Universal Pictures

Directed by George Roy Hill; screenplay by David S. Ward; cinematography by Robert Surtees; edited by William Reynolds; music by Marvin Hamlish, Scott Joplin and John Philip Sousa; produced by Tony Bill and Julia Phillips.

ABOVE
The Sting **(1973).**

■ **THE TOWERING INFERNO**
(1974) Color, 160 minutes,
Twentieth Century-Fox (U. S.),
Warner Bros. (foreign)
*Directed by John Guillermin;
screenplay by Sterling Silliphant,
based on the novels* **The Tower**
by Richard Martin Stern and
The Glass Inferno *by Thomas N.
Scortia and Frank M. Robinson;
action sequences directed by
Irwin Allen; cinematography
by Fred Koenekamp, action-
sequence photography by Joseph
Biroc; edited by Harold F. Kress
and Carl Kress; music by John
Williams; produced by Irwin
Allen.*

■ **THE DROWNING POOL**
(1976) Color, 108 minutes,
Warner Bros.
*Directed by Stuart Rosenberg;
screenplay by Tracy Keenan
Wynn, Lorenzo Semple Jr., and
Walter Hill, based on the novel
by Ross Macdonald;
cinematography by Gordon
Willis; edited by John Howard;
music by Michael Small;
produced by Lawrence Turman
and David Roster.*

■ **BUFFALO BILL AND THE
INDIANS, OR SITTING
BULL'S HISTORY LESSON**
(1976) Color, 120 minutes, a
production of the Dino De
Laurentis Corporation, Lion's
Gate Films, Inc., and Talent
Associates Norton Simon Inc.,
distributed by United Artists
*Directed and produced by Robert
Altman; screenplay by Alan
Rudolph and Robert Altman,
based on the play* **Indians** *by
Arthur Kopit; cinematography by
Paul Lohmann; edited by Peter
Appleton and Dennis Hill.*

■ **SILENT MOVIE**
(1976) Color, 86 minutes,
Twentieth Century-Fox
*Directed by Mel Brooks;
screenplay by Mel Brooks, Ron
Clark, Rudy DeLuca and Barry
Levinson, based on a story by
Ron Clark; cinematography by
Paul Lohmann; edited by John C.
Howard; music by John Morris;
produced by Michael Hertzberg.*

■ **SLAP SHOT**
(1977) Color, 123 minutes,
Universal Pictures
*Directed by George Roy Hill;
screenplay by Nancy Dowd;
cinematography by Victor J.
Kemper; edited by Dede Allen;
music by Elmer Bernstein;
produced by Robert J. Wunsch
and Stephen Friedman.*

■ **QUINTET**
(1979) Color, 110 minutes,
Twentieth Century-Fox
*Directed by Robert Altman;
screenplay by Frank Barhydt,
Patricia Resnick and Robert
Altman; cinematography by Jean
Boffety; music by Tom Pierson; a
Lion's Gate Production.*

■ **WHEN TIME RAN OUT**
(1980) Color, 121 minutes,
Warner Bros.
*Directed by James Goldstone;
screenplay by Carl Foreman and
Sterling Silliphant, based on* **The
Day the World Ended** *by
Gordon Thomas and Max Morgan
Witts; cinematography by Fred J.
Kannekamo; edited by Edward
Blery and Freeman A. Davies;
music by Lalo Schifrin; produced
by Irwin Allen.*

■ **THE SHADOW BOX**
(1980) A movie for ABC television,
December 1980
*Directed by Paul Newman;
playwright, Michael Cristofer;
produced by Paul Newman, Jill
Marti, and Susan Kendall.*

■

FORT APACHE, THE BRONX
(1981) Color, 125 minutes, a
Time-Life production released
by Twentieth Century-Fox
*Directed by Daniel Petrie;
screenplay by Heywood Gould;
produced by Martin Richards
and Tom Fiorello.*

■ **ABSENCE OF MALICE**
(1981) Color, 116 minutes,
Columbia Pictures
*Directed and produced by
Sidney Pollack; screenplay by
Kurt Luedtke; cinematography
by Owen Roizman; edited by
Sheldon Kahn; music by
Dave Grusin.*

■ **THE VERDICT**
(1982) Color, 129 minutes,
Twentieth Century-Fox
*Directed by Sidney Lumet;
screenplay by David Mamet,
based on the novel by Barry
Reed; cinematography by Andrzej
Bartkowiak; edited by Peter C.
Frank; music by Johnny Mandel;
produced by Richard D. Zanuk
and David Brown.*

■ **HARRY AND SON**
(1984) Color, 118 minutes,
Orion Pictures
Directed by Paul Newman; screen story and screenplay by Ronald L. Buck and Paul Newman; cinematography by Donald McAlpine; edited by Dede Allen; music by Henry Mancini; produced by Paul Newman and Ronald L. Buck.

■ **THE COLOR OF MONEY**
(1986) Color, 117 minutes,
Touchstone Pictures in association with Silver Screen Partners II
Directed by Martin Scorcese; screenplay by Richard Price, based on the novel by Walter Tevis; cinematography by Michael Ballhaus; edited by Thelma Schoonmaker; music by Robbie Robertson; produced by Irving Axelrad and Barbara De Fina.

■ **THE GLASS MENAGERIE**
(1987) Color, 134 minutes,
Cineplex Odeon Films
Directed by Paul Newman; playwright, Tennessee Williams; cinematography by Michael Balhaus; edited by David Ray; music by Henry Mancini; production design by Tony Walton; produced by Burtt Harris.

■ **HELLO ACTORS STUDIO**
(1987) A documentary

■ **JOHN HUSTON**
(1988) A documentary

■ **FAT MAN AND LITTLE BOY**
(1989) Color, 126 minutes,
Paramount Pictures
Directed by Roland Jaffe; screenplay by Bruce Robinson and Roland Joffe; cinematography by Vilmos Zsigmond; produced by Tony Garnett.

■ **BLAZE**
(1989) Color, 119 minutes,
Touchstone Pictures
Directed by Ron Shelton; screenplay by Ron Shelton; produced by Gil Friesen and Dale Pollock.

■ **MR. AND MRS. BRIDGE**
(1990) Color, 124 minutes,
Merchant Ivory/Robert Halmi
Directed by James Ivory; screenplay by Ruth Prawer Jhabvala, based on the novels **Mrs. Bridge** *and* **Mr. Bridge** *by Evan S. Connell; cinematograpy by Tony Pierce-Roberts; edited by Humphrey Dixon; music by Richard Robbins; produced by Ismail Merchant.*

■ **WHY HAVEL?**
(1991) A documentary

■ **THE HUDSUCKER PROXY**
(1994) Color, 111 minutes,
Warner Bros.
Directed by Joel Coen; screenplay by Ethan and Joel Coen and Sam Raimi; cinematography by Roger Deakins; edited by Thom Noble; music by Carter Burwell; produced by Ethan Coen.

■ **NOBODY'S FOOL**
(1994) Color, 112 minutes,
Paramount Pictures
Directed by Robert Benton; screenplay by Robert Benton, from the novel by Richard Russo; cinematography by John Bailey; edited by John Bloom; music by Howard Shore; produced by Scott Rudin and Arlene Donovan.

ACADEMY NOMINATIONS AND AWARDS

1958
Nominated for Best Actor
CAT ON A HOT TIN ROOF

1961
Nominated for Best Actor
THE HUSTLER

1963
Nominated for Best Actor
HUD

1967
Nominated for Best Actor
COOL HAND LUKE

1968
Nominated for Best Picture
RACHEL, RACHEL—PRODUCER

1981
Nominated for Best Actor
ABSENCE OF MALICE

1982
Nominated for Best Actor
THE VERDICT

1985
Honorary Oscar
"In recognition of his many and memorable compelling screen performances and for his personal integrity and dedication to his craft."

1986
Oscar for Best Actor
THE COLOR OF MONEY

1993
Jean Hersholt Humanitarian Award
"For his humanitarian efforts"

1994
Nominated for Best Actor
NOBODY'S FOOL

Paul Newman and several others were interviewed for this book and quotes from them are noted as "Int. with EL." Material was also drawn from articles about and interviews with him that have appeared over the past forty years, and from the Warner Bros. Pictures, Inc. (WB) Archives School of Cinema-Television, the University of Southern California (USC). The sources of these quotes are identified below.

Quotes & Notes

p.8 *"I mean, it was* wonderful." **Int. with EL.**
"Bad one ..." ibid.
"so that I could keep away from women ... Poor choice" ibid.
Degree in speech, **ibid.**
"There's some question ..." ibid.
"I was a terrible student." ibid.

p.9 *"trouble not casting Paul ..."* **Time, 6 December 1982.**
"I didn't have time ..." **Int. with EL.**

p.11 *"belligerent, I think ..."* **Playboy interview, April 1983.**
"Fierce, fierce ... all kinds of good hell." **Int. with EL.**
"I didn't know what was going on ..." **Playboy interview, April 1983**

p.13 *"I think he always thought of me as pretty much a lightweight ..."* **Time, 6 December 1982.**
"She was raised in a very poor family ..." **Playboy interview, April 1983.**
"I used to get the bejesus ..." **Time, 6 December 1982.**
"isn't a very valuable ..." ibid.

p.14 *Red and green.* **Int. with EL.**
"I wasn't all that worth tracking ... did not solidify our relationship a lot ..." **Int. with EL.**
"I don't think they ever forgave ..." ibid.
"eyeball to eyeball ..." **CBS This Morning interview with Gene Siskel, 12 January 1995.**
"The pilot I flew with ..." **Time, 6 December 1982.**
"many of them perished ..." **Int. with EL.**

p.15 *"I got through the whole war ..."* **Time, 6 December 1982.**
"I think they were generous ..." **Int. with EL.**

p.17 *"Well, let's just say ..." ibid.*
"It was a marvelous shop ..." **Saturday Evening Post, 24 February 1968.**

p.18 *Managed golf range and other jobs,* **Int. with EL.**
"I looked about four years old ..." ibid.
"I knew that I was running ..." ibid.
"the only thing I ever approached ..." **The New York Times, 9 February 1981.**
"I had no idea ..." **Player, 1962.**
"I've always considered myself ..." **The New York Times, 9 February 1981.**
"I was terrorized ..." **Time, 6 December 1982.**

p.20 *"the first thing I saw ..." ibid.*
"That performance ..." **The New York Times, 9 February 1981.**

p.22 *"When Picnic was new ..."* **The New York Times, 30 August 1953.**

p.23 *"Well, it was a very interesting performance ..."* **Playboy interview April 1983.**
"At that particular point ..." **The New York Times Magazine, 28 September 1986.**
"the way I translated ...of pursuing." ibid.

p.26 *"during my audition they mistook terror ..."* **Playboy interview, April 1983.**
"untuned piano ...my big mouth." **The New York Times Magazine, 28 September 1986.**

p.27 *"all rights ..."* **Employment agreement 8 April 1954, WB Archives, USC.**

p.30 *"almost any of the people ..."* **Int. with EL.**
Newman/Dean screen test, **WB Archives, USC.**

p.34 *"We must have smuggled ..." ibid.*
"He became a legend ..." **Int. with EL.**
"A classic example.." **The New York Times Magazine, 6 November 1966.**

p.35 *"It was fun ..."* **Time, 6 December 1982.**
Bedtime for Bonzo, **Int. with EL.**
"I feel that I didn't ..." **The New York Times, 5 May 1957.**

p.37 *"Once, in a military ..."* **Playboy interview, July 1968.**

"huge appetite has accelerated ..."
Int. with EL.
*"I didn't want to gain ..." **ibid.***

p.38 *"I tried to do ..." **Time,** 6 December 1986.*
"The actor's got to come to the part ..."
***Playboy** interview, July 1968.*
*"I almost lived ..." **ibid.***

p.39 *"Mr. Newman ...plays the role ..."*
***The New York Times,** 6 July 1956.*
"[Graziano] told me, in the only way ..."
***Playboy** interview, April 1983.*

p.41 *"I'm acting for Rocky Graziano ..."*
***The New York Daily News,** 8 July 1956.*
October 1955 Warner Bros. loaned out Newman,
WB Archives, USC.

p.42 *"to report the day following ..."*
Loan-out agreement, 2 December 1955,
WB Archives, USC.
"Brilliantly detailed performance ..."
***The New York Times,** 6 November 1956.*
"really aspired to something ..."
***Time,** 6 December 1986.*

p.44 *$2,500 loan-out fee from MGM,*
Loan-out agreement, 8 February 1957, WB
Archives, USC.
*Memo on title of The Helen Morgan Story, **ibid.***
Tested for the part. **WB Archives, USC.**
*"Uggghhh." **Time,** 6 December 1982.*

p.45 *"animal ...the true grizzly ..."*
***Playboy** interview, April 1983*
*"I always see them ..." **ibid.***

p.46 *"such peccadilloes as ..."*
***Washington Post,** 5 January 1969.*
"I've discovered ..."
***The New York Times,** 5 May 1957.*

p.47 *"The kids will never ..."*
***New York Daily News,** 5 April 1962.*

p.49 *"I stole the character ..."*
***Playboy** interview, July 1968.*
*"gives me a chance ..." **ibid.***

p.50 *"Paul Newman is best ..."*
***The New York Times,** 4 April 1958.*
He owned 14⅙ percent ... , **Agreement with**
Harroll Productions, 7 November 1956,
WB Archives, USC.
"I gave up some of my points? ..." **Int. with EL.**
*"That's like filming ..." **Collier's,** 20 July 1956.*

p.51 *"We could never get the script ..."*
***Playboy** interview, April 1983.*

p.52 *"a little bit ahead of its time ..."*
***Time,** 6 December 1982.*
"$8,000–$14,000" **Int. with EL.**
"a film that only someone ..." **Gore Vidal,**
Palmpsest, A memoir, Random House,
1995, p. 296.

p.54 *"has a real sympathy ..."*
***The New York Times,** 25 December 1994.*
"Mr. Newman is perhaps ..."
***The New York Times,** 19 September 1958.*

p.56 *"Remember Skipper, the dead friend ..."*
***New York Daily News,** 5 April 1962.*
"So you wound up with Apollo ..."
The New York Times Magazine,
28 September 1986.

p.57 *"With Joanne, you just give ..."*
***The New York Daily News,** 5 April 1962.*

p.60 *"Without her I'd be nowhere ..." **ibid.***
"I just think it was a kind of fortuitous ..."
Int. with EL.
"you should be allowed ..."
***Playboy** interview, April 1983.*
"Parked by a soundstage ..." **Int. with EL.**

p.61 *"I gave up signing autographs ..."*
***Playboy** interview, April 1983.*
*"I owe them a lot ..." **ibid.***

p.62 *"suspicious. I suppose that's why most ..." **ibid.***
*"It's simply nobody's business ..." **ibid.***

p.63 *"Paul has a sense ..." **Time,** 6 December 1982.*
"the last of the big-time broads"
***The New York Times,** 9 October 1966.*
"how incredible she is"
The New York Times Magazine,
28 September 1986.
*"If anyone had ever told me ..." **ibid.***

p.83 *"a so-called 'star dressing room' ..."*
Loan-out agreement, 5 May 1958,
WB Archives, USC.
Contract renewal, **8 August 1958,**
WB Archives, USC.
"I told Jack Warner ..."
***Playboy** interview, July 1968.*

p.84 *"half vulgar greed ..."*
***New York Herald Tribune,** 22 March 1959.*
"The three major characters ..."
***The New York Times,** 20 March 1959.*
*"brilliantly acted ..." **ibid.***
*"When Mr. Williams first ..." **ibid.***

p.86 *"I never got to know ..."* **Int. with EL.**

p.87 *"without interest by giving ..."*
Buy-out agreement, August 1959, WB Archives, USC.

p.91 *"due as much ..."*
***Playboy* interview, July 1968.**
*"Chilly." **Time**, 6 December 1982.*
"Ari Ben Canaan ..."
***The New York Times*, 16 December 1960.**

p.93 *"as though the devil ..."*
***The New York Times*, 27 September 1961.**
*"corruptibility level" **New York Daily News**,*
6 April 1962.
*"very conscious ..." **Time**, 6 December 1982.*

p.94 *"I don't think ..." **Playboy** interview,*
April 1983.
*"I was really hurt ...around to the show." **ibid.***
*"He said they'd always ..." **The New York Times Magazine**, 28 September 1986.*
*"It did ruin a great moment ..." **ibid.***

p.95 *"There are few actors ..." **Playboy** interview,*
July 1968.

p.96 *"For the first time in a long time ..." **Time**,*
6 December 1982.
*"If an actor ..." **Playboy** interview, July 1968.*

p.97 *"If I envy anything ..." **ibid.***
*"There are so many different ..." **ibid.***

p.100 *"Isn't he in show business?" **Int. with EL.***
*"When we bought the house ..." **Playboy** interview, July 1968.*

p.101 *"Three could sleep ..." **ibid.***
*"You start making ..." **Louisville Courier**, n. d.*

p.102 *"I think I probably care ..." **Int. wth EL.***

p.103 *"You could walk home ..." **ibid.***

p.105 *"You have to make peace ..." **ibid.***

p.107 *"I come back, always ..." **Playboy** interview,*
July 1968.

p.108 *"backfired. We thought the last ..." **ibid.***

p.110 *"You get to the point ..." **The New York Times Magazine**, 28 September 1986.*
*"I suppose I should ..." **Playboy** interview, July 1968.*
*"I'd be glad to ..." **The New York Times Magazine**, 28 September 1986.*
*"A real stunner ..." **The New York Times Magazine**, 28 September 1986.*

p.111 *"If you don't have a chance to rehearse ..." **The New York Times Magazine**, 12 December 1994.*
*"Joanne read it and said ..." **Time**,*
6 December 1982.

p.113 *"I liked that one." **ibid.***
"I'm not so sure that The Outrage *works ..."*
Int. with EL.
*"I woke up every morning ..." **Time**,*
6 December 1982.

p.114 *$750,000 fee and other figures from contracts,*
WB Archives, USC.
Color over black and white for Harper*, **ibid.***
*"How are ya?" **Playboy** interview, July 1968.*
*"What an extraordinary man ..." **ibid.***

p.115 *"He existed relatively intact ..." **New York Herald Tribune**, 3 April 1966.*

p.117 *"I sniffed around ..." **Playboy** interview,*
July 1968.
*"contains objectionable elements ..." **Letter**
25 May 1965, WB Archives, USC.

p.118 *"the best creative experience ..." **The New York Times Magazine**, 6 November 1966.*
*"That's the first time ..." **Int. with EL.***
*"Actors want to direct ..." **The New York Times**,*
22 October 1987.

p.119 *"I went around ..." **The New York Times**,*
1 September 1968.

p.120 *"I got involved ..." **The Times** (London),*
1968, n.d.
*"As a parent ..." **The New York Times**,*
22 October 1987.
*"I very much wanted ..." **ibid.***

p.122 *"There's a conspiracy ..." **Esquire**,*
September 1969.
*"Almost totally physical ..." **Saturday Evening Post**, 24 February 1968.*
*"As an actor ..." **The New York Times**,*
22 October 1987.

p.123 *"As Private Harry ..." **The New York Times**,*
1 March 1968.

p.127 *"Too bad they got killed ..." **Time**,*
6 December 1982.

p.148 *"a story on page nine ..." **Playboy** interview,*
July 1968.
*"I am indifferent ..." **The New York Times**,*
22 April 1968.

p.149 *"I have been fortunate ..." **The New York Times Magazine**, 1 February 1995.*
*"a film of incredible potential ..." **Time**,*
6 December 1982.
*"People in Hollywood come ..." **The New York Times Magazine**, 6 November 1966.*

p.150 *"the great relaxers in the sky" **Playboy** interview,*
April 1983.

p.151 *"Sometimes you need ..."* **The New York Times Magazine,** 6 November 1966.

p.152 *"I just decided one day ..."* **Playboy** interview, April 1983.

p.153 *"four years after Winning ..."* **Int. with EL.**

p.154 *"My racing here ..."* **The New York Times,** 11 June 1979.
"So that's why they call you ..." **Los Angeles Times,** 24 July 1985.

p.155 *"I don't care what people say ..."* **The New York Times,** 2 July 1979.
"A mind is a terrible thing to waste..." **McCall's,** January 1991.
"She has just been the best ..." **Playboy** interview, April 1983.
"Her theory is ..." **ibid.**

p.156 *"It's not a racist picture ..."* **The New York Times,** 18 April 1980.
"Sure, there are Puerto Rican ..." **The New York Times,** 9 February 1981.

p.158 *"You don't have as much wasted effort ..."* **Int. with EL.**
"the way a dog ..." **The New York Times Magazine,** 28 September 1986.
"He knew a lot ..." **ibid.**
"The emotions were there ..." **ibid.**

p.159 *"He kept trying to fake it ..."* **ibid.**
"You find some essence ..." **Int. with EL.**
"One of Paul's great strengths as an actor ..." **ibid.**

p.160 *"For a while, it really ..."* **Playboy** interview, April 1983.
"was a job I did not want ..." **Int. with EL.**
"Paul is the greatest gentleman ..." **ibid.**
"I think I made a pretty good film ..." **ibid.**

p.161 *"One of the delights ..."* **ibid.**
"Well, that has to be their problem ..." **ibid.**
"There was a wonderful Hungarian ..." **ibid.**

p.164 *"In a way, I had been ..."* **Playboy** interview, April 1983.

p.165 *"We were like rubber bands ..."* **Time,** 6 December 1982.
"There was nothing else ..." **Playboy** interview, April 1983.

p.166 *"The fact that the food ..."* **USA Today,** 27 March 1995.

p.168 *"I don't think ..."* **Int. with EL.**
"to acknowledge luck: ..." **I Will Sing Life, Voices from the Hole in the Wall Gang Camp,** by Larry Berger, Dahlia Lithwick and Seven Campers, Little Brown and Company, 1992.

p.170 *"Positive trauma" and letter,* **Int. with EL.**

p.171 *"I put a little kid on the bus ..."* **ibid.**
"It's a Paul Newman ..." **USA Today,** 27 March 1995.

p.173 *"It's about a man ..."* **Int. with EL.**
"It turned out they were interchangeable ..." **The New York Times,** 25 December 1994.

p.174 *"From an actor's point of view ..."* **Int. with EL.**
"Having written the script ..." **ibid.**

p.175 *"Robert Altman once said ..."* **ibid.**
"I wanted that Paul ..." **ibid.**
"and we got stuck ..." **ibid.**
"Sully was a lot of luck ..." **ibid.**

p.176 *"I stand between two ..."* **Thomas Mann, Death in Venice and Other Stories,** Bantam Books, 1988.

p.177 *"The bourgeois think ..."* **The New York Times Magazine,** 28 September 1986.
"Sometimes I feel it's all here ..." **The New York Times,** 9 February 1981.
"There's an old joke ..." **ibid.**
"I can't think of anything ..." **Newsweek,** 19 December 1994.

p.178 *"It's always been one of the great ..."* **Int. with EL.**

Index

ACKNOWLEDGMENTS

My thanks to Steven Koltai, Leith Adams and Peter Gardiner of Warner Bros.
and Stuart Ng and Bill Whittington of the Warner Bros. Archives School of Cinema-Television
at the University of Southern California, for access to enormously helpful material.

At Pavilion, Colin Webb had the idea, Emma Lawson and Natasha Martyn-Johns shepherded
this with a soft crook, and copy editors Annie Lee and Libby Willis expertly performed the
invisible rescues that save a writer from himself.

Juliet Brightmore tracked down and combed through thousands of photographs to select the
images, and much that is enjoyable to the eye is directly attributable to her.

Linda "Sherlock" Amster is both a wonderful friend and the most capable researcher
on earth. She adds to the pleasure of the hunt.

Carroll W. Brewster of the Hole in the Wall Gang Fund smoothed the way,
and I am very grateful to him.

My particular thanks to Paul Newman, who generously gave time to be interviewed and
graciously checked the facts for a book that he never asked to be done.

PICTURE ACKNOWLEDGMENTS

BFI Stills, Posters and Designs, London, with acknowledgment to Columbia Pictures, First Artists,
Island/Katz-Denny, Metro-Goldwyn-Mayer, Mirage Productions-Columbia Pictures, National General
Pictures, Orion Pictures Corporation, Paramount Pictures Corporation, Time-Life Productions, Touchstone
Pictures, Twentieth Century-Fox, United Artists Corporation, Universal Pictures, Warner Bros. Inc.,
Warner Bros.-Seven Arts Inc.

Robert Benson © 1992.

Camera Press, London, with acknowledgment to Dalmas, Terry O'Neill, Lawrence Schiller, David Sutton.

Joel Finler Collection, London.

Kobal Collection, London.

London Features International with acknowledgment to Sid Avery, Liefer, Ken Regan, David Sutton.

Magnum Photos, London, with acknowledgment to Eve Arnold, Magnum Group.

Newman's Own, Inc.

Pictorial Press, London, with acknowledgment to Globe, Jack Stager.

Range/Bettmann/UPI.

Rex Features, London, with acknowledgment to Globe, John R. Hamilton, Lazic, Meurou, Mooney,
Orlando, Jim Selby, Sipa Press, Irv Steinberg.

Every reasonable effort has been made to acknowledge the ownership of copyrighted photographs included
in this volume. Any errors that have inadvertently occurred will be corrected in subsequent editions
provided notification is sent to the publisher.